Diversity in the City

Diversity in the City

Edited by

Marco Martiniello
University of Liège

Brigitte Piquard
University of Louvain

2002
University of Deusto
Bilbao

No part of this publication, including the cover design, may be reproduced, stored or transmitted in any form or by and means, whether electrical, chemical, mechanical, optical, recording or photocopying, without prior permission or the publisher.

Publication printed in ecological paper

Illustration of front page: Xabi Otero

© Universidad de Deusto
   Apartado 1 - 48080 Bilbao

I.S.B.N.: 84-7485-789-9
Legal Deposit: BI - 349-02

Printed in Spain/Impreso en España

Design by: IPAR, S. Coop. - Bilbao

Printed by: Artes Gráficas Rontegui, S.A.L.

Contents

Preface 9

Introduction
Marco Martiniello (University of Liège) and Brigitte Piquard (University of Louvain)... 11

Ethnic diversity and the city
Ceri Peach (University of Oxford) 21

Citizenship and exclusion on Europe's southern frontier: the case of El Ejido
Almudena Garrido (University of Deusto) 43

When de-segregation produces stigmatisation: ethnic minorities and urban policies in France
Patrick Simon (Institut National d'Études Démographiques) 61

The study of community development in the city. Diversity as a tool
Ruth Soenen and Mac Verlot (University of Gent)............... 95

The Latinisation of the United States: social inequalities and cultural obsessions
James Cohen (University Paris-VIII) 111

Western Europe in the Urban Gap Between Mobility and Migration Flows
Barbara Verlic Christensen (University of Ljubljana)............. 135

Diasporic identities and diasporic economies: the case of minority ethnic media
Charles Husband (University of Bradford) 153

Commodity culture and South Asian transnationality
Peter Jackson (University of Sheffield)........................ 169

Preface

This book has been published within the framework of 'HumanitarianNet', the Thematic Network on Humanitarian Development Studies, which was established in 1995 with the support of the European Commission. HumanitarianNet is a network of 87 universities, 6 research centres and 9 international organizations. Its purpose is to improve the work of universities in the field of 'humanitarian development', including teaching, research, fieldwork, discussion and dissemination. Humanitarian development is conceptualised as an academic field which brings together a range of interrelated disciplines, within both the sciences and humanities, to analyse the underlying causes of humanitarian crises and formulate strategies for rehabilitation and development.

This is the third in a trilogy of books jointly produced by a subgroup of HumanitarianNet, Migration, Multiculturality and Ethnic Minorities, and the European Module on Migration, Cultural Identities and Territory in Europe. The first book, *Cultural Identities and Ethnic Minorities in Europe* (ed. D. Turton and J. González) was published in 1999. The second (Ethnic Diversity in Europe: Challenges to the Nation State) was published in 2000.

We should like to record our thanks to Mrs. Margaret Okole, of the Refugee Studies Centre, University of Oxford, for her meticulous and skilful copy-editing.

Introduction

Marco Martiniello and Brigitte Piquard

It seems the world is becoming increasingly uniform culturally. To a certain degree, this observation is correct in the sense that a global mass culture is certainly being disseminated and sold all over the planet. But the world is at the same time increasingly diversified in terms of ethno-cultural identities. The tension between the trend toward cultural uniformity and the trend toward differentiation of identities is well captured by observing the evolution of social dynamics in cities. Most medium-sized and large European cities are today increasingly fragmented socially, economically and ethnically. Some of them are even becoming socially, ethnically and racially ghettoised. But at the same time, European cities remain places where intergroup encounters can develop and where cultural production takes place. The cities are the crossroads between the local and the global.

The first aim of this book is to discuss the changes affecting the city and the role played by cultural diversity and ethno-national identities in those changes. The second aim is to examine some crucial issues and aspects of the current process of cultural diversification of cities and its impact on urban socio-economic, political and cultural activities.

In October 2000, we decided to bring together in Liège, Belgium, scholars from a large number of European universities to discuss issues linked to cultural and ethnic diversity at the city level in a multidisciplinary perspective. The aim was to form a relatively small group in a conducive atmosphere to brainstorm on the subject. Eleven papers were presented, each of them discussed by other scholars in order to feed the debate, to share approaches and views before opening the floor. Policy makers, politicians and representatives of the civil society also took part in the discussion.

This seminar was convened in the framework of the thematic network: "HumanitarianNet", and more particularly, by the subgroup on "minorities, diversity and identities". In an attempt to shed light on global burning issues, universities and research centres had joined together in 1995 in order to build up stable lines of research and teaching on issues which analyse either the causes of problematic situations or the paths to resolution, reconstruction and sustainability. The dimensions of the problems, however, and the need for centres of higher education and international organisations to join forces in searching for the best use of resources and the integration of different perspectives, called "HumanitarianNet" into being. This is a network joining a significant number of these European centres of higher education, governmental and non-governmental organisations and international associations who want to co-operate to improve the quality of knowledge and education in related subjects in the field of Humanitarian Development.

In the field of migration and ethnic studies, ten of those universities decided to create together a "European doctorate on migration, diversity and identities". This project was actually launched at the Liège seminar, though this publication is not the first initiative of the subgroup. It is in fact the last part of a trilogy. In 1999, David Turton, from the University of Oxford, and Julia Gonzalez, from the University of Deusto, edited a first volume: "Cultural Identities and Ethnic Minorities in Europe". They published a second one in 2000 on "Ethnic Diversity in Europe: Challenges to the Nation State".

The seminar in Liège was hosted by the Centre for Studies on Ethnicity and Migrations (Centre d'Études de l'Ethnicité et des Migrations, or CEDEM). CEDEM was offically created at the University of Liège in 1995, but had existed since 1991 under a different name. Its main objective is to carry out theoretical and empirical research in the fields of migration and ethnic studies. In addition to doing research, it also aims to be a forum for exchange of thoughts by delivering courses and organising seminars on issues related to ethnic studies and migration. Special attention is given to interactions with policy-makers and stakeholders on migration and ethnic issues both at the local and at the global level.

The Liège seminar also launched a closer collaboration between the University of Liège and the Catholic University of Louvain (UCL). At the Catholic University of Louvain, two centres have also been dealing with issues related to migration, ethnicity and diversity: the Groupe d'Etudes des Migrations (GREM) dealing with migration issues and particularly issues regarding Islam in Europe for the last twenty years, and the Network for Humanitarian Assisance (NOHA), created in 1995 and dealing mostly with issues related to ethnic and identity crises, forced displacement of population and responses through humanitarian actions. Together, those research centres under the name of CIM (Consortium Interuniversitaire d'Études des migrations et de la mondialisation) will offer the European doctorate in Belgium and are planning further projects in research, teaching and dissemination of results.

The choice of the city of Liège was no accident. Liège has always been a city of passage, of migration, of intercultural encounters. Due to its location at the heart of Europe and to its economic and industrial structure, Liège has for decades attracted migrants. In the nineteenth century, migrants were coming mainly from Flanders, which at the time was an underdeveloped rural area. In the interwar period, many migrants from Poland and other Eastern European countries settled in the region. Right after the Second World War, the mine industry needed an additional labour force. It came from Italy and later from Morocco as well as European countries. Nowadays, refugees and asylum-seekers from Africa and Asia live in the city and in the region.

Some people say that Liège is the most Latin city in Belgium. What is indisputable is that Liège is a multicultural, multiethnic and multiracial city with a long tradition of integration and toleration. Of course, Liège is no paradise. In this changing city, there are serious social and economic problems that sometimes find an expression in racism. But unlike in other Belgian cities, racist and fascist political parties don't play a significant role in local politics.

In any case, if we consider this long migratory history, it is not at all surprising that the University has been the cradle of migration and ethnic studies in Belgium since the 1950s. The first major surveys on migrants' assimilation were conducted in Liège by the research team led by Professor Clemens.

The guidelines given to the participants were broad. We decided nevertheless to focus on five key discussion points. First of all, the new migration patterns and the geography of the city. How do new migration inflows change the geography of the city? Secondly, the city is also a level of political regulation at which policy making is required. In a multicultural city, an important question is to what extent are the various interests represented in the political institutions. Do all individuals and groups composing the city participate in the management of the city's collective affairs? A third session discussed these questions by examining more precisely the place of ethnic minorities in the local political process: is positive action in the local polity a solution to the democratic deficit and intergroup conflict? Fourthly, we discussed the impact of migrants seen as global diasporas on socio-economic activities in the cities. New diasporas are at the interface between the local and the global. Simultaneously located in the city and in the world, they embody current economic, social and global changes. Finally, we approached the city in its culture-creating activities: what is the impact of diversity on urban cultural creation. The city is seen as a place where transnational and transcultural activities emerge, to be reflected in new forms of cultural production (cross-fertilisation, creolisation, etc.).

Three papers out of the eleven could not be published in this collection. The paper presented by Enzo Pace (University of Padova) was titled "Mazara del Vallo: from civic disregard toward the recognition of cultural difference". The analysis is conducted in three steps. First of all, it looks at the social role of an association of Tunisians in Mazara, in connection with the situation in other cities in Sicily, in order to overcome the preceding civic disregard, putting pressure on the local authority to open an immigration office in the city hall. Secondly, the efforts made by the immigrants in co-operation with the local Mazara association to organise various street parties to publicise Tunisian culture, with the aim of showing the local population the similarities and differences with the Arab world. Finally, the strategy of a group of local secondary school teachers to set up a teaching project to rediscover the Arab-Muslim cultural heritage of Mazara and Sicily in general. All these things point to a change of perspective. No longer is it the interplay of mirrored attitudes and civic disregard. The move is in another direction, to discover and rediscover ourselves toward the recognition of the cultural difference.

The second missing paper, from Wolfgang Bosswick (University of Bamberg), was entitled "From ethnic nation to universalistic immigrant integration: national developments and the local situation". The paper briefly described the background to the immigration debate in Germany and the consequences at the local level. Based on work-in-progress findings from the EU research project EFFNATIS on the integration of second generation migrant youth, the paper discussed related empirical findings from the field study in Nürnberg, Germany (see TURTON/ GONZALEZ, 2000, for related papers by Pace and Bosswick).

Finally, a third paper from Glenn Bowman (University of Kent at Canterbury), entitled "International capitalism and the inflation of the national: the case of Serbia", dealing with the new cultural expressions related to the post-war identification process in Serbia, is also not included.

The eight papers included in this volume address numerous issues which can be grouped into four main topics: immigration patterns; integration and multiculturality; ethnic spaces and territorialisation; policies.

Immigration patterns

As Ceri Peach notes, immigration in Europe follows four main patterns. First of all, a reflux of Europeans coming back from former colonies. Next, an influx of foreign workers and their families, coming first from neighbouring countries, then from the Mediterranean basin, Sub-Saharan Africa or South Asia. Then, refugees or asylum seekers, many of them coming from the former Yugoslavia and former USSR; and finally white-collar internationalists (Japanese or American transnational executives). The responses of the host population or government have varied according to the type of immigration. While the reflux created sympathy, the influx of guest workers or international white-collar workers has been neutrally accepted, according to Peach. But the flux of asylum seekers has created feelings of panic and most governments have recently been trying to repel them.

Europe has been transformed from a continent of emigration into one of immigration (THRÄNHARDT, 1992). According to Patrick Simon, this creates two strategic issues. First of all, the recognition of ethnic diversity and its impact both on social organisation and national symbolic representations. Secondly, the management of the territorialisation of social inequality. He stresses the importance of keeping in mind a dynamic view of the ethnic groups' itineraries rather then a static description of their geographical distribution.

The question of illegal immigrants, as in the case of El Ejido, is another key issue. In most European countries the real number of illegal and undocumented immigrants is unknown. Their presence is perceived as massive and uncontrolled. This leads to structural illiteracy. The situation is one of constant conflict and discrimination (Garrido). Irregular immigrants enter through contact with employers, as tourists, or as seasonal agricultural workers, and do not leave when their visa or permit expires; a minority cross the border illegally. They need to send money to their families: to make a minimum investment in housing (shanty houses) and cultural needs. Immigrants who return to their countries are normally those who have found the most success in Spain and thus have gained the means to achieve success in their own country. Immigrants in difficulties or who lose their permission to work do not go home (Garrido).

Integration and multiculturality

A first important issue discussed in this very complex debate pertains to the dangers of homogenising immigrants and ethnic minorities.

Patrick Simon and Charles Husband distinguish between the French concept of "immigrant" versus the Anglo-Saxon notion of "ethnic minority". "Immigrant" refers to individuals in terms of their foreign nationality or place of birth, without distinguishing between people of different origins. Subsequent generations born in the country are not referred to in French terminology. Dissemination or social distribution of ethnic groups in the city has rarely been used to study segregation in France (Simon).

Ethnic groups or immigrant groups are not homogeneous, though often perceived as such. Often, differences between self-definition and legal standing can be noticed (Cohen, Husband, Soenen/Verlot). Those notions invite an assumption of shared identities and histories among those caught in these labels (Husband). Charles Husband goes even further, stressing not only the diverse origins and social conditions but also the differences shaped by generation, gender or religion. James Cohen asks whether there is a Hispanic culture as such in the United States. The Hispanic community is seen as a "potent, increasingly unpredictable political force, since young Latinos are less attached to any given party then their parents". Can we talk about a Hispanic community, Cohen wonders. This is the official categorisation in the national census but it leaves aside the different origins or the different social conditions of people coming from South America. But the Latinos sometimes perceive themselves and are perceived as a community of descent, as a real ethnic block. From a political point of view, one could ask if such a community becomes a unified electoral force, especially in states and cities where it is demographically very strong (California, San Antonio). There is already a long-term political impact from the massive entry of Latinos into the exercise of US citizenship, but no opening up toward Latinos as excluded citizens or non-citizens. This can lead to a new era of social explosions in the urban areas of heavy Latino concentration, the *barrios*. The USA is an "ethno-civic" nation: "ethnic by exclusion and civic by inclusion" (Cohen).

Even though the concept of integration is highly problematic, it is still very much in use in the literature. Several negative factors for integration can be identified: the deterioration of many public housing projects (Simon); the "cohabitation" of populations whose histories and social behaviour differ significantly (Simon); the economic decline of neighbouring sources of employment (Simon, Christensen); the firm belief of employers that ethnic heterogeneity is not productive (Christensen); native voices against immigrants seen as the source of the urban crisis (Simon), etc.

Often, socio-economic cleavages are surveyed to stress the inequalities of groups of migrants who are seen as collective victims (difference in income, lower rate of employment, less educated sector, higher percentage below the poverty level (Cohen)). But alternatively, some groups can be special targets, even scapegoats: Islamic immigrants in most of the European countries (seen as competition with Christianity), but also citizens of the country, such as the gypsies in Spain (subjects of Spanish xenophobia for hundreds of years (Garrido)). This scapegoating is clearly an obstacle to integration.

The case of the anti-immigration discourses of Belgian lower-income households in some Belgian cities is a good illustration. In Antwerp, the impact of the Vlaams Blok is noticeable. The party stresses the idea that communities are built upon the sharing of the same values and daily life practices. Social and cultural diversity are seen as endangering and corrupting the basics of community (Soenen/Verlot). Such discourse also has a negative impact on integration

If complexity and diversity are key features of contemporary urban life (Soenen/Verlot), the concept of diversity is also problematic. In Jackson's view, it is too much linked to the liberal notion of multiculturalism. It fails to deal with the unequal social relations of power. Also it is related to an unexamined "core culture" whose legitimacy is rarely called into question. The notion of difference focuses more on political questions of power and inequality which leads to an examination of social relations and material practices rather than vaguely defined notions of identity and experience (Jackson).

In any case, commodity culture and transnationality provide some fresh insights into the nature of contemporary multiculturalism and diversity in the city (Jackson). There is a transformation of cultural landscapes (Peach), a progression from "soft" features of people (dress, sound) to "hard" features of building forms. Multi-ethnic populations are now a permanent part of the city and their permanence is marked by their new religious buildings (Peach). In the United States, a number of "Anglos" follow the fashion of learning about Latino culture by taking dancing lessons, Spanish classes or learning to cook Latin dishes (Cohen). According to Cohen, all groups in the USA share a common culture: the commercial culture of capitalism, the mass media, a standardised culture of fast food chains, a mass spectacle of sports (Cohen). The existence of different "ethnic markets", different "spaces of public expression" does not mean difference of interests, of values, of culture (Cohen).

Husband highlights the importance of the news media in shaping popular understandings of ethnic diversity. The mainstream media of the dominant ethnic community often tends to obscure both the existence and the importance of ethnic minority issues and media in particular (Husband). However, the "ethnic press" is very sensitive to ethnic minorities' interests.

Ethnic spaces and territorialisation

The similarity among most European countries is the fact that they adopted as a pattern of settlement, the ethnic enclave instead of the ghetto (Peach, Simon). Peach stresses the mistake of the three-generational model of the Chicago School, which fused the two models as part of the same process (a first generation ghettoised in the inner city, a second one moving out to the next urban ring, mixing with other communities and better educated, then a third generation suburbanised and homogenised with the general population).

Marc Verlot and Ruth Soenen discuss the emergence of a "nouvelle urbanité", a new suburbanisation process. In Belgium, average Belgian households moved away from the inner city in the 1960s, leaving deserted houses for guest workers. But cultural diversity still exists in more popular neighbourhoods since many Belgian families stayed there for various reasons. This avoided any form of ghettoisation.

For Peach, the black ghetto is doubly exclusive: almost entirely black, almost all blacks live in such areas. The urban enclaves are doubly diluted: minority ethnic groups only rarely form a majority in those areas, and only rarely do most of a minority group identify with a particular area.

Settlement depends on the public housing stock available (Simon). Many migrants have no choice but to settle in abandoned or insalubrious housing on the outskirts of the main French cities. Moving out of the public housing sector is perceived as a move up in the social hierarchy, while the massive presence of migrants in an area is a clear sign of its loss of prestige (Simon). Soenen and Verlot notice the same phenomenon concerning schools. The massive presence of immigrant pupils made Flemish parents remove their children from schools, fearing a decline in quality of teaching. It is only in the 1990s that the reverse development occurred with a small number of highly educated families moving into multiethnic neighbourhoods. These families consider multiculturalism an advantage. They are few in numbers but very involved in the community.

The hierarchisation between residential areas is a first sign of unequal social distribution within the urban space. It reinforces the social division of the city (Simon). Some trends can be noticed: the gentrification of the well-to-do areas on the one hand and the occupational stratification of immigrants in working class areas on the other.

Simon focuses on the importance of territorialisation as a stage in the long process of assimilation of immigrants in mainstream society. The creation of "ethnic neighbourhoods" with ethnic shops selling native foods and other products led to the development of community structures: ethnic communities in "integration neighbourhoods". This, Simon notes, is not the result of a political decision but a powerful combination of socio-economic segregation and ethnic-racial discrimination.

Space is no longer the main organising factor. There is a territorial separation between residential and commercial areas (Simon). In these conditions, social networks become very important (Simon, Soenen/Verlot). Network analysis based on the frequency of social contacts, degree of specialisation, density and range would be welcome (Soenen/Verlot)

The physical segregation of immigrants symbolises exclusion from the life of the town. The townspeople see the immigrants as workers, not as people with their own needs and cultures who live in the town (Garrido).

Policies

Integration of migrants varies from country to country. There is no consensus in Europe on the way to manage ethnic diversity (Husband). Among the European countries, we can draw two models: the assimilationist on one side (the British and French cases) or the accommodationist one (German or Swiss, accepting a wide range of migrants but denying citizenship) (Peach).

Patrick Simon, writing about the French case, describes the "code of nationality" as a formal rule requiring the active participation in society of every long-term resident, emphasising similarities, convergence, and equal rights and duties in order to preserve the cohesion of the social fabric, though different cultural features may be retained. Integration, for Simon, is seen as an individual process of admission as a citizen. Of course, there is a clash between doctrine and practice, between tolerance of difference and the "principle of undifferentiation" (Simon, Christensen).

In France as in Belgium, Simon and Soenen/Verlot note, urban policies deal only with "territories": struggle against segregation of territories and restoration of the poorest ones. Policies are designed with the idea of city renewal. In the 1970s, slum clearance programmes were carried out and migrant families were transferred to transitional housing projects ("cités de transit") where they would stay indefinitely. In France, special "Neighbourhood Social Development" programmes ("développement social des quartiers") were launched to revitalise the economic and social environment of these "disfavoured", "troubled", "sensitive" neighbourhoods (Simon). In France and in Belgium, the state is willing to create mixed areas by encouraging well-off households to move to those areas and "disfavoured" households to move to better neighbourhoods. The need to diversify the social fabric by attracting more middle and high income households has become a priority. But an influx of high income households may strengthen the process of social exclusion (Soenen/Verlot).

The field of education has also been the subject of policy-making. Intercultural education has not altered the social and cultural relations between "newcomers" and "settled pupils" (Soenen/Verlot). Often the specific approach to immigrant pupils came down to setting them apart and applying a more intensive and specific programme to acquaint them with the "school culture". Immigrants' cultural background was seen as detrimental to their chances of success in the education system. There was a change in the 1990s: increasingly, these social and cultural features are taken into account and perceived as valuable differences (Soenen/Verlot).

Obviously, this volume does not pretend to provide solutions for all the questions raised by the various authors. It nevertheless presents insights into the issues of diversity in the city which are important for policy making and policy implementation.

References

THRÄNHARDT, D. (Ed.) (1992): *Europe: A new Immigration Continent. Policies and Politics in Comparative Perspective*, LIT Verlag, Münster-Hamburg.

TURTON, D.; GONZALEZ, J. (1999): *Cultural Identities and Ethnic Minorities in Europe*, HumanitarianNet, University of Deusto Press, Bilbao.

TURTON, D.; GONZALEZ, J. (2000): *Ethnic Diversity in Europe: Challenges to the Nation State*, HumanitarianNet, University of Deusto Press, Bilbao.

Ethnic diversity and the city

Ceri Peach

The period 1945 to 1996 saw a net movement of about 33 million migrants and refugees across international borders in western Europe. By way of comparison, in the period 1820 to 1985, there was a net migration of about 56 million people into the USA. The population of Europe is larger than that of the USA in the period in which most of the US migration was taking place, but the impact in demographic and psychological terms on Europe, a continent that was previously thought of as an exporter of population, has been considerable.

The post-war period in Europe has seen four main waves of inward immigration:

—*Reflux* of Europeans (1945-1974) from their colonial territories overseas or from their areas of historic settlement in Eastern Europe. The main groups were Germans arriving from Slavic lands, French from North Africa, Dutch from Indonesia and British from their colonies. About 16 million such people exist or existed.
—*Influx* of worker and family immigration 1950-1999, caused by expanding economies and ageing populations in Europe. Typified by Turks moving to Germany, Algerians to France, West Indians and South Asians to Britain, in 1993 there were about 12 million in western Europe and by the late 1990s closer to 20 million.
—*Refuge* 1989-2000. The new wave of asylum seekers from the former Socialist bloc —the former USSR, Yugoslavia— as well as the dispossessed from earlier Islamic upheavals in Iran, Afghanistan, Iraq, Kurdistan and Algeria, civil wars in Sri Lanka, Somalia, Rwanda and Burundi and elsewhere.
—Fourthly, we have seen the growth of the two newish movements of white-collar internationalists; the chess pieces of transnationalism, Japanese and Americans parachuted into corporate city slots.

Alongside them are Europeans on the move, settling for a while in other people's countries. Paul White, for example, writes how the French have given a distinctive flavour to a part of Kensington in London, playfully dubbed "frog valley" alongside the young Australians' "kangaroo valley" (WHITE, 1998a, 1988b).
—Finally, there have been lifestyle developments, particularly in the display of sexuality and the formation of gay villages, which have added to the diversity of the city. However, space does not allow us to develop this theme.

Post-war Western Europe has experienced a demographic shock. The continent which considered itself to be an exporter of population has found itself to be the destination of substantial waves of immigration. While the causes and consequences of these movements are complex and contested, this paper attempts an overview of the major contributory factors.

Whereas the political response to reflux was sympathy and the response to influx was neutral acceptance, the reaction to asylum seekers and refugees has been closer to panic. Western Europe is battening down the hatches and trying to repel potential refugee seekers. At the same time, there are profound differences in the strategies adopted by different countries in their acceptance or denial of their new minority ethnic populations. There are also powerful political conjunctions in the movements: the populations of the reflux form the hard core of the right wing opposition to influx and efflux.

Reflux

In this phase, involving movement of Germans from Slavic lands, French from North Africa, Dutch from Indonesia and British from their colonies, the largest number of returnees and expellees came to Germany. The Potsdam post-war settlement removed East Prussia and severed Silesia from Germany, allocating these territories to the USSR and Poland. Ethnic Germans were expelled from these areas and those, such as Sudetenland, which had been annexed by Germany during the war. The Soviet Zone of Germany was eventually created the new state of the German Democratic Republic. It is thought that between 1945 and 1960, 9 million Germans fled to West Germany from the annexed territories. Between 1945 and the building of the Berlin Wall in 1961, it is thought that a further 3 million East Germans fled west. Altogether, about 12 million Germans fled to the west.

In addition to these directly displaced or fleeing people, there was a continuous stream of ethnic Germans (*Volksdeutsche*) whom the Federal Republic virtually bought from the East European states, where they had been settled for hundreds of years. Anyone with German ancestry was entitled to come. Thus groups like the Silesian Poles, who had relatives in the German army in the past, for example, could claim German citizenship. Poland, Rumania and the USSR had considerable populations of ethnic Germans. As conditions in the Socialist countries deteriorated, the numbers moving to Germany increased substantially. Between 1968 and 1984, 652,897 ethnic Germans moved to the Federal Republic. From 1985 to 1991, a further 1,332,829 settled. Thus, from 1968 to 1991, nearly 2 million ethnic Germans moved to Germany, in addition to the 12 million discussed above in the earlier phase. These ethnic German arrivals in Germany are known as *Aussiedler*.

Table 1. *Aussiedler* in Germany according to countries of origin, 1968-1991

	Poland	ex USSR	Bulgaria	Yugo-slavia	Rumania	Czecho-slovakia	Hungary	Other	Total
1968-1984	365,234	72,664	195	9,982	147,528	47,011	7,065	3,218	652,897
1985	22,075	460	7	191	14,924	757	485	69	38,968
1986	27,188	753	5	182	13,130	882	584	64	42,788
1987	48,419	14,488	12	156	13,990	835	579	44	78,523
1988	140,226	47,572	9	223	12,902	949	763	29	202,673
1989	250,340	98,134	46	1,469	23,387	2,027	1,618	34	377,055
1990	113,253	147,455	27	530	107,189	1,324	1,038	11	370,827
1991	40,129	147,320	12	450	32,178	927	952	27	221,995
Total	1,006,864	528,846	313	13,183	365,228	54,712	13,084	3,496	1,985,726

Source: *Statistisches Jahrbuch, 1992, für die Bundesrepublik Deutschland*, table 3.39, p. 91.

Return movement to other European countries has been on a totally different scale from that of Germany. In 1962, after Algerian independence, there was a mass return of about 1 million *pieds noirs*, French settlers in that country (GUILLON, 1974). The Netherlands experienced a return flow of about 250,000 to 300,000 Dutch and Indonesians in 1953, when Indonesia became independent. In a few years up to 1975, when Surinam became a separate state, about 104,000 Surinamese left for the Netherlands in order to claim Dutch rather than Surinamese citizenship (PEACH, 1991, p. 20-21). However, this latter movement is not an ethnic return movement in the sense of the German and French movements. In 1975 after Angolan independence from Portugal, about 400,000 Portuguese settlers fled that country, a substantial proportion returning to their native country. Settler return to Britain has undoubtedly occurred, but not in the dramatic way of the cases mentioned so far. The 1991 census shows that of the 1,653,002 born in the New Commonwealth, that is to say former colonial territories, living in Great Britain, 328,080 (or 20 per cent) were white. Together with 250,000 whites from Australia, New Zealand, Canada and South Africa, this made over half a million whites from the Commonwealth. In western Europe, these reflux migrants have generally been quietly absorbed, although they may have had important political effects in some cases in their support for right wing parties.

Influx: worker migration

1945-1990

However, when one refers to immigration in Europe, it is the worker movement which is assumed to be the focus of attention. Although earlier movements had taken place, such as the Polish worker migration to the northern coal fields of France in the 1920s and 1930s, the post-war movement of labour into Europe was a revolutionary change of direction from the previous patterns of migration affecting the continent. Between 1950 and 1975, worker migration to western Europe, together with dependants, grew from practically nothing to about 12 million. Table 2 (next page) shows the position for some of the largest groups in 1990 for selected west European countries

This table should be read in two directions: (1) along the bottom rows and (2) down the final column. Reading along the bottom rows, Belgium has nearly 1 million foreigners, about 40 per cent of whom come from outside the EC; France has 3.6 million of whom two thirds are non-EC. Germany has the largest number of foreigners of whom two thirds originate from outside the EC. Seven eighths of the 1.5 million foreigners in the Netherlands are non-EC and two thirds of the British total of 2 million overseas origin population are non-EC. Reading down the final column, the largest individual source of migrants into Europe is Turkey with 2.6 million (three quarters of whom are in Germany); Italy is the next largest supplier with 1.5 million (over a third of whom are in Germany, but with substantial numbers in Switzerland, Belgium and France). Morocco, rather surprisingly, has more citizens overseas than Algeria, 1 million as opposed to 650,000, but both

Table 2: Major sources and destinations of international immigrants to Western Europe (thousands), late 1990s

Country of Origin	1997 Belgium	1990 France	1997 Germany	1997 Nether-lands	1998 UK	1997 Switzer-land	1997 Italy	1997 Spain	TOTAL
Turkey	73.8	197.7	2,107.40	172.7	63	79.6			**2,694.2**
Algeria	8.9	614.2	23.1						646.2
Morocco	132.8	572.7	82.8	145.8			131.4	111.1	**1,176.6**
Tunisia	4.7	206	28.1	1.5			48.9		289.2
Iran			101.5	16.5					118
Afghanistan			30						30
Pakistan			17		69				86
Bangladesh			23		69				92
India			12		139				171
Caribbean				183.2	122				305.2
Former Yugoslavia		52.5	721	46.7		313.5	14.3	5.7	**1,178.1**
Bosnia-Herzegovina			281.4				44.4		**281.4**
Croatia			206.6						**206.6**
Poland	6		283.3				31.3		320.6
Italy	295.8	252.8	607.9	17.4	89	342.3		22.6	**1,627.8**
Spain	47.4	216	131.6	17.6		94	17		523.6
Portugal	25.3	649.7	132.3	8.7		136.5		38.2	**990.7**
Greece	10.2		362.5	5.3		6.4	16.5		394.5
Ireland	19.5				448	55			473.9
France	103.6		103.9		74	94.7	28.3	34.3	415.6
Germany	33.3				75	218.8	40.1	49.9	419.8
Other	141.9	835	2,110.40	790.3	918		868.5	238	6,120.9
TOTAL	**903.2**	**3,596.6**	**7,365.80**	**1,549**	**2,066**	**1,340.8**	**1,240.7**	**499.8**	**18,561.9**

Source: SOPEMI, 1999

heavily concentrated in France. Portugal, with almost 1 million citizens in western Europe, particularly France, is the other major supplier of note.

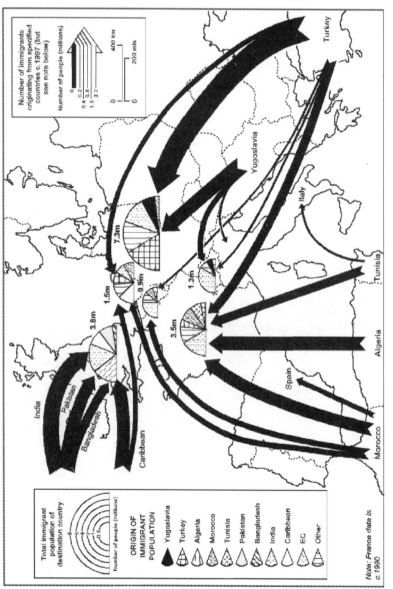

1950-1973

Essentially the period of worker migration divides into the explosive growth stage, between 1950 and the oil crisis of 1973, and the period of entrenchment and family reunification from 1973 until the present. By 1973, there were about 15 million foreign immigrants living in the industrialised countries of north-west Europe. Their numbers remained stable at that level until 1983 and since that time have shown a decrease. The period from 1945 to 1973 witnessed a massive increase in immigration as the European economies recovered from the war. The recovery manifested itself earliest in Britain and France, with Germany acting as a source of immigrants until the early 1950s. German demand for foreign labour grew from just over 100,000 in 1958 to over 1 million in 1966. By 1968, Germany had overtaken France as the largest concentration of foreign labour (MÜHLGASSNER, 1984, p. 73).

In France and Germany, immigration took place as a result of planned bilateral agreements between those governments and third parties[1]. In Britain and the Netherlands, the movement was largely unplanned, although specific industries and services made initiatives which were important beyond the scope of directly involved authorities (PEACH, 1991).

Essentially, what happened during the period 1945 to 1973 was that there was an outward ripple effect in terms of the catchment area of migration to western Europe. In the period up to the late 1950s, the movement was dominated by local effects —migration from adjacent or close countries: Irish to Britain, Finns to Sweden, Italians to Switzerland, France and Germany and so on. In the later period, to 1973 and beyond, the ripples extended far beyond the European catchment to include the Mediterranean basin, sub-Saharan Africa and South Asia.

---

[1] France set up a national immigration office (ONI) in 1945 and thereafter concluded a series of bilateral agreements with different governments. Between 1945 and 1950, agreements were made for the recruitment of German and Italian workers. Further agreements were made with Greece (1954), Spain (1961), Morocco, Tunisia, Portugal, Mali and Mauritania (1963), Senegal (1964), Yugoslavia and Turkey (1965). These arrangements were in addition to the supply of Algerian labour, freely available before independence in 1962 and which continued thereafter. Germany concluded bilateral arrangements with Italy (1955), Spain and Greece (1960), Turkey (1961), Morocco (1963), Portugal (1964), Tunisia (1965) and Yugoslavia (1968) (PEACH, 1992, p. 116).

Within this perimeter, there was a geographical partitioning of territory. The Mediterranean basin was effectively divided along the axis of Italy into a western French sphere of influence and an eastern German sphere. The Maghreb and sub-Saharan Africa, Spain and Portugal fell into the French sphere. Yugoslavia, Greece and Turkey fell into the German sphere and Italy was divided between the two. Countries such as Austria and Switzerland showed a German pattern of migration sources. Belgium followed a more French pattern.

There was, in addition, a British pattern which was of overseas flows from former colonial territories in the Caribbean and South Asia. The Dutch shared some of the characteristics of the British pattern and some of those of the German (see map 1).

1974-1993

This rapid expansion of immigration into western Europe was brought to a dramatic halt by the oil crises of 1973/1974. The Yom Kippur War and the consequent rapid rise of oil prices following the Arab countries' embargo on exports, produced a major dislocation in western economies. Both France and Germany imposed a halt on immigration and tried to make migrants return to their home countries. Between 1974 and 1981, the overall number of foreigners living in Europe stabilised. Generally speaking, the number of workers decreased while the number of dependants increased. For example, between 1973 and 1981 the number of foreign workers in Germany decreased from 2,416,000 to 2,096,000 and in France from 1,813,000 to 1,600,000. On the other hand, the total foreign population increased from 4,127,000 in Germany to 4,630,000 and in France from 4,043,000 to 4,148,000 (PEACH, 1987, p. 36).

The period since 1974 has seen the maturing of many of the immigrant groups, so that, with some of the earliest established communities, the sex ratios have become more even and the majority of the ethnic minority population have been born in the countries of settlement. We are no longer talking about simple immigrant minorities. Taking the sex ratio first, in Britain in the 1991 census, the numbers of Caribbean born men and women are almost identical. The number of Indian born women slightly exceeds that of Indian born men (1,055 women per 1,000 men). For more recently arrived groups such as the Bangladeshis, the ratio was 883 women per 1,000 Bangladesh-born men. In Germany the ratio of Turkish women per 1,000 Turkish men rose from 554 in 1974 to 856 in 1989 (SOPEMI, 1990, p. 143). Although it is difficult to establish what proportion of

Turks have been born in Germany, 41 per cent were under 18 years of age at the time of the 1987 census, compared with 17 per cent for the German population as a whole. In France in 1985, there were 701 Algerian women per 1,000 Algerian men (SOPEMI, 1990, p. 145) indicating a continuing substantial imbalance of the sexes.

The new wave: post-1988 asylum seekers

Europe 1985-1991

In the period leading up to and following the fall of the Berlin Wall and the associated collapse of socialist systems in Eastern Europe, there was a substantial growth in the number of asylum seekers moving into western Europe from the East. In 1983, there were less than 54,000 but in 1991, the annual figure reached nearly half a million (see Table 3). The overwhelming majority of these asylum seekers moved to Germany, whose constitution obliged the government to accept them. In 1991,

Table 3. Inflows of asylum seekers into selected European countries, 1980-1998 (thousands)

	Belgium	Denmark	France	Germany	Greece	Italy	Netherlands	UK	Sweden	Total
1980	2.7	0.2	18.8	107.8			1.3	9.9		140.7
1981	2.4	0.3	19.8	49.4			0.8	2.9		75.6
1982	3.1	0.3	22.5	37.2			1.2	4.2		68.5
1983	2.9	0.3	22.3	19.7	0.5	3.1	2	4.3	4	59.1
1984	3.7	4.3	21.6	35.3	0.8	4.6	2.6	4.2	12	89.1
1985	5.3	8.7	28.8	73.8	1.4	5.4	5.6	6.2	14.5	149.7
1986	7.6	9.3	26.2	99.7	4.3	6.5	5.9	5.7	14.6	179.8
1987	6	2.7	27.6	57.4	6.3	11	13.5	5.9	18.1	148.5
1988	4.5	4.7	34.3	103.1	9.3	1.4	7.5	5.7	19.6	190.1
1989	8.1	4.6	61.4	121.3	6.5	2.2	13.9	16.8	30	264.8
1990	13	5.3	54.7	193.1	4.1	4.7	21.2	30.2	29.4	355.7
1991	15.4	4.6	47.4	256.1	2.7	27	21.6	73.4	27.4	475.6
1992	17.3	13.9	28.9	438.2	2	2.6	20.3	32.3	84	639.5
1993	26.2	17.1	27.6	322.6	0.8	1.3	35.4	28.5	37.6	497.1
1994	14.7	6.7	26	127.3		1.8	52.6	42.2	18.6	289.9
1995	11.7	5.1	20.4	127.9	1.4	1.7	29.3	55 9	261.5	
1996	12.4	5.9	17.4	116.4	1.4	0.7	22.9	375.8	219.9	
1997	11.8	5.1	21.4	104.4	4.4	1.9	34.4	41.5	9.6	234.5
1998	22	5.7	21.8	98.7	2.6	4.7	45.2	79.8	13	293.5
	190.8	104.8	548.9	2,489.4	48.5	80.6	337.2	485.7	347.2	4,633.1

Source: SOPEMI, 1997, 1998 and 1999 editions

the number of asylum seekers in Germany reached over a quarter of a million. The political pressure to repeal this provision was intense and in 1993, all-party agreement to do so was secured.

Movement into Southern Europe and the Schengen Agreement

Until the late 1980s, attention on worker migration and asylum seeking was focused on northern Europe. However, in the late 1980s immigration into southern Europe became a notable phenomenon. Table 3 shows that Greece and Italy, which had not figured on the tables of refugees before 1983, began to register arrivals in that year. Restrictions on immigration had been progressively tightened in northern Europe, beginning with British legislation in the 1962 Commonwealth Immigrants Act, but becoming most clear with German and French legislation to halt worker migration in the aftermath of the 1973 oil crisis. Southern Europe, however, which had been an exporter rather than a receiver of immigration, had no comparable legislation.

Since the mid 1980s migrants from North and sub-Saharan Africa have been arriving, often illegally, in Italy, Spain and Portugal. Because southern European countries had traditionally been exporters rather than importers of labour, arrivals were not subjected to rigorous immigration controls. However, as those controls tightened in northern Europe, the south became an easier point of access. The Schengen agreement allows for the free movement of populations without passports between the signatory states within the EC. Thus, once across the external boundaries of the Community, movement of the undocumented becomes difficult to control. Italy began to regularise its illegal immigrants in 1987 (SOPEMI, 1990, p. 21). Of these, the largest group at the end of 1990 came from North Africa and sub-Saharan Africa (80,000 Moroccans, 41,000 Tunisians and 25,000 Senegalese) but there were also 30,000 Yugoslavs and 34,000 Filipinos. In 1991, Italy had a sudden influx of about 38,000 Albanian refugees. About 17,000 of them were immediately repatriated (SOPEMI, 1992, p. 66). There was also a sharp increase (from 99,509 in 1989 to 238,365 in 1990) in the number of residence permits granted to foreigners from Africa (largely North Africans).

Spain has, in recent years, received what have been called the 'new wetbacks'. The original wetbacks were the Mexicans who entered the USA illegally over the Rio Grande. The new wetbacks come across the Straits of Gibraltar, in frail fishing craft, and are often made to swim the last dangerous stretch. Some do not make it. Between 1989 and

1992, 36 bodies were found by the Spanish authorities on either side of Tarifa, in the main entry zone (*The Economist*, 12 September 1992, p. 56). In 1985 and 1986, Spain mounted an operation to regularise illegal immigrants and again in 1991. About 40 per cent of the 100,000 or so who were successful, were Moroccan. In 1991, Spain introduced visa requirements for citizens of Maghreb countries (SOPEMI, 1992, p. 77).

Western Europe has changed from a subcontinent of emigration to a subcontinent of immigration. It has changed from a set of countries which between 1918 and 1945 sought to make themselves internally more homogeneous, into a set of countries with dramatically changed ethnic compositions. The chillingly labelled process of "ethnic cleansing" in the former socialist states of eastern Europe has a major potential to add to this change in the west. The migration frontiers of Europe have changed during the 1990s from the south to the east. The south continues to send migrants, but they are coming to the countries of southern Europe.

The process of absorption of the new minorities is very different in the main receiving countries. There are, I believe, two main types: (1) the assimilationist model of the British, the French and the Dutch; and (2) the accommodationist model of the Germans and the Swiss. This is a bold generalisation which hides many differences between countries placed in the same categories, but which nevertheless, holds important truths.

The assimilationist model stems from the colonial histories of the British, French and Dutch. Trapped by their own political rhetoric, they gave citizenship and/or voting rights to many of their colonial subjects. They did not expect any but the elite to use their rights to gain access to the metropolitan countries. The political integration of minorities into those states has been achieved, since to an extent the right to vote had been granted before the minorities arrived.

The accommodationist model of the Germans is fraught with greater difficulties. The Turkish minority is large and well established. The second generation is substantial and German educated. However, with reunification, with the continued inflow of the *Aussiedler*, the inflow of asylum seekers wished upon Germany by an imposed post-war constitution, coupled with a deep economic depression, the political forces ranged against giving citizenship to Turks born in Germany are substantial.

The focus of this paper is the worker migration; data on asylum seekers and their settlement in European countries is more recent and less well known. The earliest movement was into Britain starting in

1948 and later into France and Germany. Thence it has spread to fill in the Benelux countries, Switzerland and Austria. From there it has spread to the Nordic countries and now to the southern Atlantic and Mediterranean shores, with Portugal, Spain, Italy and Greece becoming the new front door of Europe.

What has been the impact of these flows on the cities themselves? Despite the different ethnic groups involved, despite the different numbers and proportions formed by these groups, despite the different constitutional positions of the minority population in the various countries, despite the different time-scales over which the movements have taken place, there is an overriding similarity of the patterns of settlement between the European countries. Not only is there a commonality of pattern, but that pattern is not that of the African American ghetto. It is the pattern of the ethnic enclave.

To begin with, we need to understand the difference between the ghetto and the enclave. The Chicago School made a massive mistake when it fused these two models into a single type. The Chicago School was based on what we can call the *three generation model*. The first generation was geographically concentrated and socially ghettoised in the inner city. It did not speak the language, was employed at the lowest levels, was uneducated and married its own kind. The second generation moved out of the inner city to the next urban ring. It was better educated, spoke the English language in America, improved economically; moved up socially and out geographically. It began marrying out. The third generation was suburbanised and homogenised with the general population. It was spatially mixed with the core society and assimilated socially.

The problem with this three generational model was that it assumed that the ghetto was part of the general model and not a distinctive spatial formation in its own right. In the Chicago School model, the second generation ethnic enclave was conceptualised as a low-fat version of the first generation ghetto —the same, but a bit less concentrated. In reality, the first generation was never ghettoised in the way in which the black population was ghettoised.

The key difference between the black ghetto and the urban enclave was that the ghetto was doubly exclusive. Black areas were almost entirely black; almost all blacks lived in such areas. Ethnic enclaves, on the other hand, were doubly dilute. Minority ethnic groups only rarely even formed a majority of the population of the areas with which they were identified; only rarely did a majority of the minorities identified with particular areas (their so-called 'ghettos') live in such areas. Thomas Philpott's *The Ghetto and the Slum* (1978) demonstrates the point for Chicago in 1930 at the end of the era of mass migration (table 4).

Table 4. 'Ghettoisation' of ethnic groups, Chicago, 1930

Group	Group's City Population	Group's 'Ghetto' Population	Total 'Ghetto' Population	Percentage of group 'Ghettoised'	Group's percentage 'Ghetto' Population
Irish	169,568	4,993	14,595	2.9	33.8
German	377,975	53,821	169,649	14.2	31.7
Swedish	140,913	21,581	88,749	15.3	24.3
Russian	169,736	63,416	149,208	37.4	42.5
Czech	122,089	53,301	169,550	43.7	31.4
Italian	181,861	90,407	195,736	49.7	46.2
Polish	401,316	248,024	457,146	61.0	54.3
Negro	233,903	216,846	266,051	**92.7**	**81.5**

Source: PHILPOTT (1978, p. 141, table 7)

It can be seen that while the African American population formed 81.5 per cent of the population of the black ghetto and while 92.7 per cent of the black population lived in the black ghetto, only 3 per cent of the Irish lived in Irish areas and they formed only one third of the population of Irish areas. The two most concentrated white groups were the Italians and the Poles. Just under half of the Italians lived in Italian areas and they formed just under half of the the population of Italian areas. The Poles were a little more concentrated: 61 per cent lived in Polish areas and they formed just over half of the population of Polish areas.

However, even their levels of concentration were different in kind rather than different in degree from the situation of African Americans. All the European minorities lived in mixed areas. Hardly any of the blacks did. While white ethnic enclaves dissolved over time, black ghettos intensified and expanded territorially in a compact form.

European attempts to understand minority settlement in their cities as the American ghetto model are entirely misplaced. The model of the ghetto and the model of the ethnic enclave are totally different in kind, in form, in origin and in their futures. Europe has enclaves, not ghettos. To give an example, if we examine the concentration of minority ethnic groups in London in the 1991 census, along the lines of the Chicago table, we find that black groups look much more like the Irish in Chicago in 1930 than like the African Americans (table 5).

Table 5. 'Ghettoisation' of ethnic groups at ED level in Greater London: 30 per cent cutoff

Group	Group's City Population	Group's 'Ghetto' Population	Total 'Ghetto' Population	Percentage of group 'Ghettoised'	Group's percentage 'Ghetto' Population
Non-white	1,346,119	721,873	1,589,476	53.6	45.4
Black Caribbean	290,968	7,755	22,545	2.6	34.4
Black African	163,635	3,176	8,899	2.0	35.6
Black Other	80,613				
Indian	347,091	88,887	202,135	25.6	44.0
Pakistani	87,816	1,182	3,359	1.4	35.2
Bangladeshi	85,738	28,280	55,500	33.0	51.0
Chinese	56,579	38	111	0.0	34.2
Other Asian	112,807	176	572	0.2	30.8
Other Other	120,872	209	530	0.2	39.4
Irish born	256,470	1,023	2,574	0.4	39.8

Source: PEACH, 1996.

It is not even that the US levels of concentration and segregation for African Americans have decreased substantially since 1930. If we examine the proportion of African Americans in Chicago living in areas where they form a high percentage of the area's population, we find the same situation holding as it did in 1930. Of the total black population of 1.3 million living in Chicago PMSA in 1990, 88 per cent were living in areas which were 30 per cent or more black (cf. the London figures for the 30 per cent cut off in table 2); 82 per cent were living in areas which were half or more black. Two thirds were living in areas which were 90 per cent black; 29 per cent were living in areas which were 99 per cent or more black and 8 per cent were living in areas 100 per cent black (table 6).

The levels of segregation of African Americans in the US are such that they have been termed 'hypersegregated' by MASSEY/DENTON (1993).

In a way, the American and the European literature has been dominated too much by the index of dissimilarity (ID) and has paid too little attention to the absolute levels of concentration of minority groups. Recent advances in the European literature allow us to look in a broadly comparative way at levels of segregation in different European countries. O'LOUGHLIN/GLEBE (1987) led the way with their 1987 volume *Immigrants in West European Cities*. Complete issues of *Tijdschrift voor Sociale en Economische Geografie* and of *Urban Studies*

Table 6. Percentage of the African American population of Chicago PMSA in 1990, living in tracts of a given black percentage

Black Percentage of Tract	Black Population living in such tracts	Percentage of the total Black Population of Chicago in such tracts
100 per cent	111,804	8.4
99 per cent or more	381,347	28.7
90 per cent or more	884,725	66.5
50 per cent or more	1,087,600	81.7
30 per cent or more	1,163,969	87.5
Total Black Population	1,330,636	

Source: Based on data from GeoLytics Census CD+Maps US Census 1990 data www.GeoLytics.com

were devoted to an analysis of the levels of segregation of minority populations.

In addition, MUSTERD/OSTENDORF/BREEBART (1998) have synthesised and systematised measurements of segregation for Amsterdam, Brussels, Frankfurt, Düsseldorf, London and Manchester. They show that North Africans in continental Europe and South Asians in Britain manifest the highest levels of segregation of the composite groups which they consider (Amsterdam 40, Brussels 60, Düsseldorf 25, Frankfurt 18, London 44, Manchester 49). While these figures are not exceptionally high, Musterd et al.'s methodology of aggregating minorities into 'South Asian' and 'North African' groups disguises some of the critical factors. Bangladeshis in Britain have an exceptionally high rate of segregation, averaging 73 on the Index of Dissimilarity across the 11 cities in which they numbered 1,000 or more in 1991 (PEACH, 1996, table 9), while Pakistanis averaged 61. Nevertheless, European rates of segregation are moderate when compared with those of African Americans.

Britain as a model for future European experience

To some extent we can use the UK experience as a predictor of future developments elsewhere in Europe. The UK was the earliest country to experience large-scale non-European immigration. In this respect, it was ten years in advance of Germany, so that there is a longer track record here than elsewhere. On the other hand, most of Britain's immigrant population came from its former colonial areas and had the right to vote and the option of British citizenship. This marks a major difference between them and, say, the Turks in Germany.

The British experience is of two main immigrant groups: those of Afro-Caribbean and other African origin, and the South Asian descendants. There are sharp differences both within and between these groups. However, one can detect two basic models of accommodation to British society: the Irish model and the Jewish model.

Although the Afro-Caribbean population has a notably more blue-collar socio-economic profile than the white population and has a higher proportion living in social housing than the white population, it has nevertheless achieved significant upward economic mobility and shows a significant degree of intermarriage and co-habitation with the white population (table 7). In addition, the mean unweighted average Index of Dissimilarity (ID) for the Caribbean population compared with whites in the 17 cities where more than 1,000 Caribbean population were living in 1991, was 45 (PEACH, 1996, table 11). In Greater London, which contained just under 60 per cent of the British Caribbean population, the ID at ward level had shown a continuous decrease between 1961 and 1991 from 56 to 41 as outward suburbanisation took place (PEACH, 1996, table 13).

The South Asian populations (Indians, Pakistanis and Bangladeshis) all show far greater social closure. All three groups show a strong preference for arranged marriages, for married couple households and extended families. However, while their social conventions show strong similarities of traditional family values, their economic fortunes differ considerably. The Indian population has a white collar profile comparable to that of the white population and indeed rather higher in the professional class (ROBINSON, 1996) while the Pakistani and to a greater extent the Bangladeshi population is more blue collared, coupled with a low rate of female participation in the formal labour market. All three groups have higher average IDs from whites than do the Caribbeans. The most segregated are the Bangladeshis with an average unweighted ID of 73; the Pakistanis have an average index of 61 with whites and for the Indians, the ID with whites was 45, just slightly higher than for the Caribbean/white comparison.

However, while the Caribbean population was showing trends of decreasing concentration, all three South Asian groups indicated the opposite trend. Indeed, it was notable for the Indian population, with its white collar distribution, that suburbanisation did not equate to dispersal, as in the Chicago three generational model. It followed much more what I have termed the pluralist model of voluntary segregation.

Table 7. Ethnic marriage and co-habitation patterns, Britain 1991
Unions expressed as percentage of male's ethnic group

	White	Black Caribbean	Black African	Black Other	Indian	Pakistani	Bangla-deshi	Chinese	Other Asian	Other Other	Total %	Total
White	**99.49**	0.08	0.03	0.05	0.06	0.01	0.00	0.06	0.12	0.11	100	126,803
Black Caribbean	27.27	**67.76**	0.97	1.21	0.48	0.24	0.00	0.24	0.36	1.45	100	825
Black African	17.08	5.69	**74.02**	1.42	0.71	0.36	0.00	0.00	0.00	0.71	100	281
Black Other	51.70	2.04	1.36	**42.18**	0.68	0.00	0.00	0.00	1.36	0.68	100	147
Indian	6.93	0.10	0.21	0.05	**91.06**	0.93	0.00	0.26	0.21	0.26	100	1,935
Pakistani	5.05	0.00	0.00	0.12	0.72	**93.26**	0.00	0.00	0.48	0.36	100	831
Bangladeshi	3.00	0.00	0.86	0.00	1.72	0.43	**93.13**	0.00	0.00	0.86	100	233
Chinese	12.59	0.00	0.00	0.00	0.74	0.00	0.00	**86.67**	0.00	0.00	100	270
Other Asian	14.71	1.07	0.27	0.27	1.07	1.07	0.27	0.53	**79.14**	1.60	100	374
Other Other	**50.46**	0.46	0.23	0.46	1.62	0.93	0.00	0.46	1.16	**44.21**	100	432
												132,131

France, Germany, Belgium and the Netherlands

There has been a surge of publications on France, Germany, Belgium and the Netherlands since the pioneering effort produced by John O'LOUGHLIN and Günther GLEBE in 1987. Since then the literature has expanded substantially and in the last three years there have been two issues of major journals, *Tijdschrift voor Economische en Sociale Geografie*, 1997 and *Urban Studies* 1998 (vol. 35) devoted to analysis of the position of minority ethnic populations in a European context. MUSTERD *et al.* (1998) have also sought to synthesise and systematise these researches into a single volume.

Despite the fact that the precise composition of ethnic minorities, the history of their movement and the constitutional situations of minorities vary very considerably between European countries, there are nevertheless some over-riding similarities.

—Migrant workers have been drawn in as a replacement population for jobs which the native population was avoiding. They have filled gaps in the occupational and housing structures.
—The movement has generally been to large cities.
—The movement has generally been to the depressed parts of large cities, though these locations have not always been inner cities. In France, for example, it has been predominantly to *les banlieus*, the high rise social housing on the periphery. In Amsterdam, the suburban Bijlmermeer seems to have become depressed *as a result of* minority settlement.
—Although the American black ghetto model has been universally invoked by the press to represent the settlement patterns, in reality these patterns follow what I have termed the ethnic enclave or urban village model rather than the dual characteristics of the black ghetto.
—There are areas where minorities form a high percentage of the local population, but they do not constitute a majority of the population over large areas. (The highest proportion that minorities formed at District level in Cologne in 1995 was 50.6 per cent (FRIEDRICHS, 1998, p. 1758).)
—Nor do high percentages of minority populations live in areas where they form a majority.
—Taking the Index of Dissimilarity at the level of ward, tracts or *Stadtteile* (about 12,000 persons) as a guide, and benchmarking the values <39 as low; <59 as moderate and >60 as high, we find that the overwhelming majority fall into the moderate to low category.

—Among the high categories are two opposite extremes: very poor, very recent Muslim populations such as the Bangladeshis in Britain; and rich short-sojourners like the Japanese in London and Düsseldorf.

Cultural landscapes

Finally, we come to the transformation of cultural landscapes. If we think of the diversity of the city, we can see a chronological development from the arrival of non-European faces, different clothes, different languages and music, different shops selling unfamiliar goods in the early days to the arrival of new building forms in the later days. In other words, there has been a progression in the cultural landscape from the soft features of people, dress and sound to the new, hard features of building forms. This latter development is particularly associated with the Islamicisation of the worker and ayslum-seeking populations and is possibly further advanced in Britain than elsewhere in Europe, because of the longer period of settlement.

A project has been run in Oxford over the last three years examining the growth of Muslim mosques, Hindu temples and Sikh gurdwaras. There are about 1,000 such places of worship which are officially registered in England and Wales and possibly double that number if the smaller unofficial domestic places of worship were to be included. Altogether, the official listing of places of worship for Muslims, Sikhs and Hindus in England and Wales amounts to just under 1,000 buildings. Of these, only about 200 or 20 per cent are purpose-built, but about half of these, or about 10 per cent of the whole, are both purpose-built and decorated. Some of them are of cathedral size and make a huge impact on the cultural landscape. The contested nature of some of these buildings can be seen from the severe modulation of their characteristic features. Minarets, in some cases, appear as almost the prehensile representation of a former feature. Cupolas are sometimes understated. Building materials fit in with the surrounding styles.

Even so, these buildings are more confident and self-assertive than mosques in German cities. In Düsseldorf, where there are many Turkish families, mosques tend to be located out of sight, in courtyards. Mosques, gurdwaras and mandirs are the concrete representation of a self-confident multi-cultural society. We have passed the stage of soft additions to the cultural landscape and are now in the era of the concrete.

Conclusion

Minorities now form a significant proportion of the population of large European cities. In Frankfurt am Main they formed 30 per cent in 1995, in Düsseldorf, Cologne and Munich (FRIEDRICHS, 1998) and London, for example, they formed about 20 per cent of the population. Multi-ethnic populations are now a permanent part of the city and their permanence is marked by their new religious buildings.

Yet European cities are diverse in their particular patterns, in the combination of ethnicities, in the availability of social housing, private rentals and the locations of housing (KESTELOOT/VAN WEESEP/WHITE, 1997). In many ways, KESTELOOT and VAN DER HAEGEN (1997) show that Brussels has a very different pattern of settlement from other cities. AMERSFOORT and CORTIE's (1973) and AMERSFOORT and KLERK's (1987) work on Amsterdam also shows very distinctive patterns of a suburbanised working class ethnic Surinamese minority.

Yet despite these high percentages and relative recency of settlement, they do not seem to be moving on the American black ghetto model. ID Levels of segregation for groups in aggregate or taken singly are generally below 60. Even where groups are above 70, as is the case for Bangladeshis in Britain and Turks in some German cities and Brussels, they do not form the majority of population of large areas and the proportion living at high densities is generally below 50 per cent of the group.

One theme that unites the experience of European cities and the minority populations is a growing Islamicisation of the minority, both workers and asylum seekers. This, together with a dissatisfaction with the dry statistical approach, is leading us to a greater appreciation of life-styles, life worlds and cultural landscape. It offers another line of unifying pan-European approaches to minorities and diversity in cities. There are, of course, many different schools of Islam.

In a general sense, then, European cities show some similarities amongst themselves in comparison to the African American model. There are similarities to the process that has been observed historically with regard to other American minorities.

We have seen the growth of privileged new sojourner groups as well as the well-known labour immigrants. The Japanese are significant for their high levels of spatial segregation, yet at the same time they teach us that we should not get too worried about high levels of ID. There are positive reasons for groups wishing to stick together as well as the negative reasons that have received the largest amount of attention

References

AMERSFOORT, H. VAN; CORTIE, C. (1973): "Het Patroon van de Surinamse vestiging in Amsterdam 1868 t/m 1970". In: *Tijdschrift voor Economische en Sociale Geografie*, 64, pp. 283-94.
AMERSFOORT, H. VAN; DE KLERK, L. (1987): "Dynamics of Immigrant Settlement: Surinamese, Turks and Moroccans in Amsterdam 1973-1983". In: *Immigrants in West European Cities*, ed. John O'Loughlin and Günther Glebe. Franz Steiner Verlag, Stuttgart.
BURGERS, J. (1998): "In the Margin of the Welfare State: Labour Market Position and Housing Conditions of Undocumented Immigrants in Rotterdam". In: *Urban Studies* 35, pp. 1855-1868.
DALEY, P.O. (1998): "Black Africans in Great Britain: Spatial Concentration and Segregation". In: *Urban Studies* 35(10), pp. 1703-1724.
FRIEDRICHS, J. (1998): "Ethnic Segregation in Cologne, Germany, 1984-1994". In: *Urban Studies* 35(10), pp. 1745-1764.
GIFFINGER, R. (1998): "Segregation in Vienna: Impact of Market Barriers and Rent Regulations". In: *Urban Studies* 35, pp. 1791-1812.
GLEBE, G. (1986): "Segregation and Intra-Urban Mobility of a High-Status Ethnic Group: The Case of the Japanese in Düsseldorf". In: *Ethnic and Racial Studies*, 9, pp. 461-483.
GUILLON, M. (1974): "Les rapatriés d'Algérie dans la région parisienne". In: *Annales de Géographie*, 83, pp. 644-675.
KEMPEN, R. VAN; ÖZÜEKREN, A.S. (1998): "Ethnic Segregation in Cities: New Forms and Explanations in a Dynamic World". In: *Urban Studies* 35(10), pp. 1631-1656.
KEMPEN, R. VAN; WEESEP, J. VAN (1998) "Ethnic Residential Patterns in Dutch Cities: Backgrounds, Shifts and Consequences". In: *Urban Studies* 35, pp. 1813-1834.
KEMPER, F.-J. (1998): "Restructuring of Housing and Ethnic Segregation: Recent Developments in Berlin". In: *Urban Studies* 35, pp. 1765-1790.
KESTELOOT, C.; CORTIE, C. (1998): "Housing Turks and Moroccans in Brussels and Amsterdam: The Difference Between Public And Private Markets". In *Urban Studies* 35, pp. 1835-1854.
KESTELOOT, C.; WEESEP, J. VAN; WHITE, P. (1997): "Introduction to the Special Issue on Minorities in West European Cities". In: *Tijdschrift voor Economische en Sociale Geografie*, 88(2), pp. 99-104.
KESTELOOT, C.; HAEGEN, H. VAN DER (1997): "Foreigners in Brussels 1981-1991: Spatial Continuity and Social Change". In *Tijdschrift voor Economische en Sociale Geografie*, 88(2), p. 119.
LEE, T. R. (1973): *Race and Residence: The Concentration and Dispersal of Immigrants in London*. Clarendon Press, Oxford.
MÜHLGASSNER, D. (1984): "Der Wanderungsprozess". In: *Gastarbeiter: Leben in zwei Gesellschaften*, ed. E. Lichtenberger. Bohlau Verlag, Wien.
MUSTERD, S.; OSTENDORF, W.; BREEBART, M. (1998): *Multi-ethnic Metropolis: Patterns and Policies*. Kluwer Academic Publishers, Dordrecht.

O'LOUGHLIN, J.; GLEBE, G. (Eds) (1987): *Immigrants in West European Cities*. Franz Steiner Verlag, Stuttgart.
PEACH, C. (1987): "Immigration and Segregation in Western Europe since 1945". In: *Immigrants in West European Cities*, ed. John O'Loughlin and Günther Glebe. Franz Steiner Verlag, Stuttgart.
PEACH, C. (1991): *The Caribbean in Europe: Contrasting Pattern of Migration and Settlement in Britain, France and the Netherlands*, Research Paper in Ethnic Relations 15, Centre for Research in Ethnic Relations, University of Warwick.
PEACH, C. (1996b): "Does Britain have ghettos?" *Transactions of the Institute of British Geographers*, 22(1), pp. 216-235.
PEACH, C. (1997): "Postwar Migration to Europe: Reflux, Influx, Refuge". In: *Social Science Quarterly*, 78(2), pp. 269-283.
PEACH, C. (1998): "South Asian and Caribbean Minority Housing Choices in Britain". In: *Urban Studies* 35(10), pp. 1657-1680.
PEACH, C. (1999): "London and New York: Contrasts in British and American Models of Segregation". In: *International Journal of Population Geography*, 5, pp. 319-351.
PHILLIPS, D. (1998): "Black Minority Ethnic Concentration, Segregation and Dispersal in Britain". In: *Urban Studies* 35(10), pp. 1681-1702.
PHILPOTT, T.L. (1978): *The Slum and the Ghetto*. Oxford University Press, New York.
ROBINSON, V. (1986): *Settlers, Transients and Refugees*. Clarendon Press, Oxford.
SOPEMI (various years) *Trends in International Migration: Continuous Recording System on Migration*. Organisation for Economic Co-operation and Development, Paris.
WHITE, P. (1998a) "The Settlement Pattern of Developed World Migrants in London". In: *Urban Studies* 35(10), pp. 1725-1744.
WHITE, P. (1988b) "Skilled International Migrants and Urban Structure in Western Europe". In: *Geoforum*, 19, pp. 411-422.
WOODS R.I. (1976): "Aspects of the scale problem in the Calculation of Segregation indices, London and Birmingham, 1961 and 1971". In: *Tijdschrift voor Economische en Sociale Geografie*, 67(3), pp. 169-174.

Citizenship and exclusion on Europe's southern frontier: the case of El Ejido

Almudena Garrido

El Ejido: a savage "miracle"

What happened in El Ejido?

On 5 February 2000, in the marketplace of Santa Maria del Águila in El Ejido,[1] Almeria, Spain, a Spanish woman was attacked and killed by a Moroccan immigrant armed with a knife. The previous day the Moroccan had been treated for mental illness. After the news of the killing spread, many of the 48,000 Spanish inhabitants of El Ejido massed on the streets of the town with sticks, stones, knives, iron bars and baseball bats. They blocked the main roads and began to attack Moroccans in the town's shops and streets.

The Spanish central government delegate for Andalucia came to El Ejido with 150 national police, but their presence did not prevent the violence from unfolding. After the woman's funeral, the crowd began to riot, destroying the town's mosque, bars, halal butchers, restaurants, telephone centres and cars belonging to Moroccans. In the outskirts of El Ejido, where the immigrants lived dispersed in farm buildings, usually in degrading conditions, trucks began to arrive full of people from the town who drove the immigrants off and burnt and destroyed everything in their path. According to the report by SOS Racismo (2001), from which some of the facts in this article are drawn, the absence and inactivity of the police were notable. The violent acts were not limited to attacks on immigrants: reporters, politicians and organisations working with immigrants were also affected.

In all 55 persons were arrested and 23 imprisoned: 12 Moroccans and 11 Spaniards. The violence continued for 72 hours before fizzling out on Tuesday 8 February.

---

[1] The Spanish *El Ejido* translates as "The common land".

Some background to El Ejido

El Ejido, in the province of Almeria, is located in a direct line across the Mediterranean from the Spanish enclave of Melilla on the North African coast. Its history is marked by immigration. In 1963, when the first plastic greenhouse was erected, the municipality had a population of 2,000 inhabitants. By the year 2000, the registered population had risen to some 50,000 of whom 8% were legal immigrants. However, there was an unknown number of illegal immigrants living around the town. The change was caused by a revolution in the methods of intensive farming under plastic, which is often referred to as the "El Ejido miracle" and which spread to other areas nearby such as La Mojonera, Roquetas del Mar, Vicar, Nijar and Campohermoso.

Most immigrants, however, come to work in the plastic greenhouses. They are frequently undocumented and without any type of work contract. They live in terrible conditions, often in old agricultural buildings (cortijos) without running water or sanitation, and in their work are exposed to dangerous levels of pesticides and other agricultural chemicals. In the last three years there has been an increase in the number of family groups of immigrants, with the number of children tripling. There is an almost complete lack of infrastructure to cope with these immigrants and very little action by institutions. The situation is one of constant conflict and discrimination.

El Ejido, the "heart of the plastic", has 50 banks, 50 women's hairdressers, and not many newsagents or bookshops. There are unknown numbers of undocumented immigrants, and continually increasing investment in the plastic greenhouses to continue growth. There is enough acreage of plastic in Almeria to cover Manhattan three times.

One major group of immigrants is made up of Russian women, who are drawn to work as hostesses in night-clubs and strip-clubs, often shading into prostitution. There is a high rate of divorce among local couples. To the women of El Ejido, naming Russian women is like naming the devil. On the other hand, a graffito seen in El Ejido reportedly demanded menos moros, mas rusas —"Less Moors, more Russians".

What were the immediate reactions and consequences?

On 17 February 2000 the European Parliament condemned the murder and the racist events which had taken place in El Ejido (Almeria), demanding from the government a total solution, applying the commitments made in Tampere.² This was the second time in the last ten years that the European Parliament had made a pronouncement on racial events in the EU Community. The first time was in 1992 when neo-nazi groups attacked immigrants in the German towns of Rostock and Lidedenhagen.

For many days newspapers, web pages, and the general public, in a state of shock, debated the events, their causes, and the prior warnings of people like Marrakesh-based novelist and reporter Juan Goytisolo, and philosopher and political scientist Sami Nair MEP, who described El Ejido in terms such as "the El Dorado of clandestine work and of overexploitation"³. As early as 1985 Ubaldo Martinez Veiga denounced the exploitative character of the Almerian "miracle".

On the other hand, Juan Enciso (mayor of El Ejido) blamed the immigrants for the violence, saying, "The foreigners have to adapt to the culture of the country, they have to respect the country. The Moroccans don't respect it, they assemble in houses, bother the neighbours."⁴ He proposed restricting the proportion of Moroccan immigrants and increasing the number of other, more "docile" immigrants from Latin America and Eastern Europe.

The stereotype of Moroccans as aggressive and problematic is reinforced by the workers' reaction against their labour situation and extreme vulnerability to exploitation. Furthermore, landowners are afraid of the Moroccan workers organising themselves and demanding their labour rights, causing them to lose the pool of extremely cheap labour on which the El Ejido "miracle" is founded.

The central government spoke of the need to reform the Immigration Law (Ley de Extranjeria), to regularise immigration because "an undocumented immigrant does not exist for the government and thus it is not easy to come to their aid." The government linked the aggression to a hypothetical increase in irregular immigrants, thus evading institutional responsibility for the situation that had existed for years in El Ejido.

The situation in El Ejido has not been resolved. The situation now is little different than it was before the violent events of February 2000. The effect has nonetheless been profound on the public image of immigration in Spain and across Europe.

---

² The European Council held a special meeting on 15 and 16 October 1999 in Tampere on the creation of an area of freedom, security and justice in the European Union.
³ "Contra la razon de la fuerza", *El Pais,* 10 February 2000.
⁴ "Bienvenidos al paraiso: milagro almeriense", TVE Channel 2, 1 November 2000.

The events of El Ejido shocked and surprised Europeans who were used to thinking of Europe as a civilised and safe haven for immigrants. It also focused the spotlight of attention on the situation of immigrants in Spain, and illegal immigrants in particular. Prior to El Ejido, immigration in Spain was barely perceived, and if it was, was not seen as a big issue. Since El Ejido, immigration is one of the top items on the political agenda and reports appear frequently on TV and in newspapers. Most of these reports, however, focus on the drama of illegal immigrants crossing the Mediterranean in open boats or being arrested at ports. Is this a realistic perception of immigrants in Spain today, and what are the results of and responses to immigration?

Immigrants in Spain: who, where, from where, how and doing what?

Legal immigrants

Since the start of the 1980s, a new-found prosperity has made Spain the destination for a wave of immigrants from Europe and beyond. Spain's entry to the EU and its ratification of the Schengen Agreement in 1994 opened the way for the free circulation and residence of EU citizens. Although they do not appear on the evening news, the largest single class of immigrants to Spain consists of EU citizens exercising their right to live and work in another Member State.

As of 31 December 1999, the number of foreigners with residence permits or an identity card in Spain was 801,332. This figure has increased by a factor of 4 since 1981, and now stands at about 2 % of the total population.

The media image suggests that most immigrants come from poor countries. The figures, however, do not bear this out. 52 % of legal immigrants are under the community regime (immigrants from the EU resident in Spain, and relatives of EU and South American citizens), while 48 % are under the general regime (non-EU immigrants with residence permits who are employed or self-employed in Spain). These numbers do not include the majority of pensioners who are not registered, "Arab Sheikhs" (millionaires of Arab origin who have mansions on the Mediterranean coast) or irregular immigrants. Of the "top six" nations with the greatest numbers of immigrants to Spain, only one (Morocco) is outside the EU.

The highest concentrations of immigrants are still in the tourist areas on the Mediterranean coast and the islands —Baleares (5.1 %),

Tenerife (4.9 %). However, density is increasing in industrial (Madrid, Barcelona) and agricultural (Almeria) provinces. Immigrants are located differently according to their countries of origin. In Madrid and Barcelona and in agricultural areas, more than half are from outside Europe. In Murcia 65 % are from Africa. In tourist areas on the Mediterranean, however, most are from Europe. In the Baleares 76 % are from Europe. Thus there is evidence of ethnic differentiation in the location of specific migrant communities in particular areas, and fulfilling particular functions in the labour market. At its crudest, "Eastern European" migrants provide essential cheap labour in the service industries, whilst "non-European" migrants have been disproportionately employed in a variety of forms of manual labour. The former have contact with the majority population through their employment, whilst the latter tend not to.

More than half the immigrants —54 %— are male. Among Africans, the percentage of men rises to 70 %. On the other hand among Latin Americans, between 60 % and 75 % are women, depending on country of origin. There is occupational segregation for women, as all the different activities are dominated by men except for domestic service

Among immigrants from Europe and North America, the retired (over 65 years) are a substantial group (more than 15 %). Among those from Africa and Latin America, however, young people are a major group.

In relation to the social system 58 % of legal immigrants are registered with social security —which gives an estimate of the number that are engaged in economic activity. The main sectors of employment are agriculture and fishing (33 %), construction and domestic service (15 % each), hotels and catering (11 %) and self-employment (6 %). These figures, however, only cover legally registered immigrants. [5]

Irregular immigrants

A una ciudad del norte yo me fui a trabajar	To a city in the north I went to work
Mi vida la dejé entre Ceuta y Gibraltar	My life I left between Ceuta and Gibraltar
Soy una raya en el mar, fantasma en la ciudad	I'm a drop in the ocean, a ghost in the city
Mi vida va prohibida dice la autoridad	My life's forbidden, say the authorities

---

[5] Observatorio Permanente de la Inmigración, numbers obtained from Anuario Estadistico de Extranjería, Comisaria General de Extranjería y Documentación (Dirección General de la Policía, Ministerio de la Interior).

Mano negra, clandestino	'Black' worker, clandestine
Peruano, clandestino	Peruvian, clandestine
Africano, clandestino	African, clandestine
Marijuana, ilegal	Marijuana, illegal
Solo voy con mi pena, sola va mi condena	I'm alone with my sadness, condemned to exile
Correré mi destino, para burlar la ley	I'll risk my life to fool the law
Perdido en el corazón de la grande Babylon	Lost in the heart of the great *Babylon*
Me dicen el clandestino por no llevar papel	They call me clandestine for having no papers
Me dicen el clandestino, yo soy el quebraley	They call me clandestine, I'm the lawbreaker
Argelino, clandestino	Algerian, clandestine
Nigeriano, clandestino	Nigerian, clandestine
Boliviano, clandestino	Bolivian, clandestine
Mano negra, ilegal	'Black' worker, illegal

Manu Chao, "Clandestino"

Figures for illegal immigrants, by their nature, are much more difficult to obtain and less accurate than those for legal immigrants. They are like marijuana and other illicit drugs: existing everywhere, but visible nowhere. A relevant figure is that of deportations. In 1999, a total of 20,103 orders to deport foreigners from Spain were issued, of which 16,928 were carried out.[6] Clearly this can only be a small proportion of those actually resident.

The first group of "irregular" immigrants, mostly Moroccans, who came to the agricultural areas to work did not arrive in open boats ("pateras") but rather through contacts made with employers. They entered the country without papers and were legalised by obtaining residence permits though the system of "convocatoria de contingentes", under which annual quotas for the entry of new immigrants are determined by the Spanish government. These "contingents" can sometimes serve to regularise the status of people already living in the country. Subsequently, the number of immigrants from the Maghreb grew as production increased, and as auxiliary industries developed. The Plan for Rural Employment was responsible for improving the conditions of indigenous agricultural labourers, and resulted in higher concentrations of people from the other side of the Mediterranean, who were the only ones prepared to work long hours in hard

---

[6] Delegación del Gobierno para la Extranjería y la Inmigración.

conditions. Their lack of papers made them vulnerable and willing to accept low-paid jobs. According to "Almeria Acoge", the main organisation dealing with irregular immigrants in Almeria, the majority of the present irregular immigrant population do have temporary work permits but do not have residence permits. In many cases, however, they have only a verbal contract.

Even when these immigrants do have contracts, the need to send money to their families left behind in Africa makes them accept a style of life with high densities of occupation in sub-standard, often unsanitary housing, spatially excluded from the life of Spanish cities and towns.

The dramatic and spectacular arrival of undocumented immigrants is a frequent item on television news: in fragile boats, in the hold of a freighter, or in containers. Most, however, do not arrive in this way, but as tourists, with the relevant visa, who then stay in Spain without a residence permit; or else come with seasonal permission and don't leave. That is not to say that those much-televised modes of immigration are not important and tragic.

The organisations which traffic in people are trying to maximise their profit, as we can observe from the fact that, in just twelve months, the average number of people transported on each of the open boats intercepted by the Civil Guard has more than doubled. According to the data provided by the Department of the Interior, in the first nine months of 2000, security forces intercepted a total of 365 boats with 7,833 immigrants on board. In 1999 the number of boats intercepted was 400, but they carried only 3,569 people, less than half the 2000 total. The consequences are easy to imagine: 42 deaths between January and September 2000, compared with 29 for the previous year; and 47 disappearances, twice as many as 1999. As the associations of immigrants affirm, the data do not include corpses gathered by the Moroccan authorities in their territorial waters nor those who disappear in this zone. On the other hand, the data of the ministry do not agree with those of the Civil Guard of Tarifa, which has recorded 263 corpses taken from the sea since the start of the year[7].

The reason for the spectacular increase in the number of immigrants in 2000 must partly be that until February of that year sub-Saharan immigrants did not arrive in boats, but entered from the camps of Calamocarro, Ceuta and la Granja, Melilla. There they obtained provisional residence permits and crossed legally to the

---

[7] Antonio Izquierdo in *La Vanguardia*, 4 October 2000.

Peninsula. Since the Government has closed this channel, large numbers of sub-Saharan immigrants now use open boats.

In any case, the data provided by the Department of the Interior only refer to the interceptions of open boats. To these must be added the boats that dump the immigrants a few metres from the coast and return with impunity to Morocco. Many are taken prisoner when they have been in Spain for some hours or days. The total number of immigrants arrested in Andalusia in the first nine months of 2000, according to the Delegation of the Government in Sevilla, comes to 10,983, compared with 5,492 in the whole of 1999.

Aside from certain temporary factors, such as the special process of regularisation that ended on 31 July 2000, the rate of arrival of immigrants seems to be on the increase. A Civil Guard report predicts a continuing increase in migratory pressure, which will not stabilise for some years. The demographic factor will be decisive. By 2025, it is projected that the European population will have stabilised at around 700 million inhabitants, whereas the African population will be more than 1,400 million.

In one sense, the reason for the increasing number of immigrants in Spain is because more new immigrants are arriving than are returning to their countries of origin. This may not be because they want to stay in Spain. As Izquierdo (1996) explains, the immigrants who return to their countries are normally those who have found the most success in Spain, and thus have gained the means to achieve success in their own country. There has thus been little response to incentives offered to immigrants to return to their countries. Immigrants who lose their permission to work do not go home: they simply lose the right to go to the labour market on an equal basis with other workers. The rejection of renewal of work permits has no relation to regulating the total volume of immigrants in Spain: it only affects the amount of abuse that the immigrants will suffer.

As Nkembo Manzambi, president of the "Afrovasca" Refugees and Immigrants Association, points out during an interview "documentation is the basic problem of irregular immigrants. Without papers, you don't exist. You don't have a single right: neither work, housing, nor health care. Your life is taken away and, if caught by the police, you can be expelled immediately." Documentation is the only means of integration available to immigrants, and consequently is of immeasurable importance to them. The "papers" have a magical aura and take on the role of a fetish object. This paper fetish works as a powerful means of social control on behalf of the government. Consultants have appeared who seek to profit from this situation by charging large fees to assist immigrants in the regularisation of their papers.

What is the law on immigrants in Spain?

The first Immigration Law (Ley de Extranjeria) was passed by the Spanish parliament in 1985, against much opposition from unions, human rights associations, anti-racist and immigrant organisations, due to its stringent restrictions on the rights of immigrants.

Due to the rising number of immigrants, and the perceived need to accept and regularise an existing reality, a new law came into force on 11 January 2000, which recognised the rights of those irregular immigrants who could prove that they were already in Spain on 1 June 1999, giving them the opportunity to legalise their residency. It also permitted regularisation of those who had applied for a residence or work permit, or who had held this permit, within the last three years. A total of 246,089 immigrants applied for permits through this "extraordinary process of regularisation", of which 137,454 applications were successful.

The argument of the Spanish government in recent years has been that "We cannot have a law which encourages a greater number of immigrants to come to our country." The high visibility given to immigration by the media following El Ejido, in particular the pictures of illegal immigrants trying to cross the Straits of Gibraltar in open boats, led the government to believe that the country was under serious threat from immigration; although, as we have seen, in reality a small minority of immigrants arrive in this dramatic fashion. It has been said that another factor involved was the "call effect" (efecto llamada) of the regularisation process: the publicity linked to the granting of papers to immigrants already present in Spain, attracted many more thousands to attempt to cross the borders, legally or illegally.

In consequence, the government passed a new, much stricter immigration law, which came into force on 23 January 2001, provoking demonstrations and hunger strikes by immigrants. A motion claiming the unconstitutionality of this law was passed by the regional parliament of the Basque Country. This new law is much more restrictive with regard to the fundamental rights of undocumented immigrants. It denies them the rights of demonstration and assembly, even the right to belong to a union. It also provides for the expulsion of illegal immigrants within a period of 48 hours, and restricts the right of asylum, as well as providing sanctions against those who harbour or transport illegal immigrants. This law has been widely criticised as an example of institutionalised racism. As Nkembo Manzambi of Afrovasca says, "there are two types of racism: the type we suffer in the street, due to the fear of foreigners, which can be cured; and the racism of the institutions, that of the Law of Immigration, which has no cure.

What is the extent and impact of racism in Spanish society?

> Nations that attain a high level of material and cultural prosperity are at a perilous moment in their history. These nations come to suffer from a grave amnesia, they forget human pain, their civilisation becomes superficial.
>
> Antonio Machado

The events of El Ejido are the tip of an iceberg in Europe: the structural exploitation of foreign workers as the basis of certain sectors of the economy, including that of intensive agriculture. Racism manifests itself in various ways, both institutional and social, expressed in this sector as legal exclusion and physical segregation.

On the legal side, employers practise fraudulent contracting to avoid giving continuous contracts to workers even though the system of greenhouse cultivation requires a continuous workforce. The limited number of legal immigrants permitted by the government encourages continuation of the irregularity.

Discrimination in access to employment, and government policy, have made the legal situation of immigrant workers depend on the fluctuations of the labour market. The granting and renewal of residence permits is tied to the possession of an employment contract. Since there is an official priority of employment for native workers, work contracts are only given to immigrants for those occupations in which the supply of local manual labour is insufficient.

Another manifestation of institutional racism is the inactivity of the police when faced with aggression against immigrants. This was clearly noted in El Ejido but is in fact widespread.

Physical segregation of immigrants symbolises exclusion from the life of the town. The townspeople see the immigrants as workers, not as people with their own needs and cultures who live in the town. Segregation means invisibility. Significantly, in El Ejido in February 2000 it was exactly those immigrants who were most integrated —who had businesses in the town, who had married local women— who were attacked with the greatest hatred. This reflects a strong fear on the part of natives that the immigrants will "escape" from the ghetto to which they have been consigned.

Segregation affects not only housing but also education. In many Spanish cities the majority of the children of immigrants are concentrated in a small number of "ghetto" schools.

According to Abdelhamid Beyuki, president of ATIME (Association of Moroccan Immigrant Workers in Spain), xenophobia is on the rise in

Spain, and is closely related to the images of illegal immigrants transmitted by the media, as well as to the message projected by both governments and opposition parties in order to justify their migration policies. The result is a general and systematic rejection of immigrants by society.[8]

This is not a situation peculiar to Spain. Each year sees a greater number of cases of racial violence, discrimination and crimes by neo-nazi groups throughout the EU. A third of Europeans consider themselves to be "very" or "quite" racist, and the Eurobarometer considers that the reasons for the increase in xenophobia are principally fear of unemployment, insecurity, general worsening in social conditions and mistrust of government policies.[9]

Of all immigrant groups in Spain, racism seems to be most strongly directed against those from the Maghreb, of which Moroccans bear the brunt. This sentiment is particularly marked in Andalucia, as shown in the comments of El Ejido's mayor blaming Moroccans for the violence in El Ejido —comments which, incidentally, did not meet with any rebuke from his party at regional or national level.

It is important to realise also that racism in Spain is not only directed against immigrants. A group even more marginalised than irregular workers from the Maghreb, if that is possible, is the gypsies. According to the NGO Presencia Gitana (Gypsy Presence), there are around one million gypsies in Spain, including 70,000 each in Barcelona, Madrid and Granada. Their level of education is very low, while their population growth is unusually high (almost 5 % per year, compared with a Spanish average of less than 1 %). They are subject to both artificial dispersal (expulsion from their habitual places of residence causing breakage of social ties) and forcible residence in ghetto areas. In surveys of racism, gypsies are said to be the group that is the object of most discrimination: more than 50 % of Spaniards are said to show prejudice against gypsies.[10] All this is despite the fact that they are Spanish citizens and have been living in Spain as a group for hundreds of years.

Clearly racism has deep roots in Spanish society and positive action is necessary to promote integration. What, in fact, is being done?

---

[8] Interview, *Consumer* magazine, February 2001.
[9] European Observatory on Racism and Xenophobia, Vienna.
[10] Los españoles y la inmigracion. Colección Observatorio Permanente de la Inmigracion.

What has been done to promote integration of immigrants?

There are around 850,000 non-European immigrants in Spain, almost four times the figure ten years ago. Among these the irregular imigrants may constitute as many as 300,000. How does Spanish society try to promote the integration of these immigrants?

The main action on integration proposed by the central government is under the "GRECO" programme.[11] This is a collection of 72 proposals intended to be implemented over the period 2001-2004. As yet none of these actions have been implemented on a national level. Most of the proposals concern policing or administrative procedures; the few actions proposed relating to integration include:

—Limited provision of health care to certain classes of resident foreigners
—Special courses for immigrant children to assist their integration in the education system
—Simplified procedures to aid regrouping of immigrant families
—Facilitation of the constitutionally guaranteed right to religious freedom
Improvement of naturalisation procedures

On an educational level the principal problems of integration detected in the immigrant pupils were:

—The lack of previous education
Lack of linguistic skill
Cultural disorientation
—Religious conflicts (food, schedules, calendar, etc.)
Conditions of life

The Department of Education, together with the Autonomous Communities, is preparing a State Plan of Educational Attention to Immigrant Pupils, elaborating a register by nationality and educational level in each autonomous community, since the education of the immigrant population is different in each Spanish territory. The creation of a programme of specific teacher training is also foreseen.

Also in the area of education, a government-funded pilot project in a school in Almeria has attracted attention. As reported in an article in *El País* (10 June 2001), the school of Las Lomas in Roquetas del Mar has begun to reach out to the children of newly arrived immigrants

---

[11] A global programme to regulate and co-ordinate foreign residents' affairs and immigration in Spain. Immigration Department, Ministry of Internal Affairs.

through the ATAL (Temporary Linguistic Adaptation Classroom) programme. The aim of this introductory course, lasting a maximum of three months, is to prepare these children to become part of the educational system —avoiding the need to lower the standard of instruction once they join regular classes— but also to teach them how to live in Spanish society.

At the regional level, Catalonia provides the most notable model for integration. Important measures taken include a policy of housing immigrants in urban areas, not in the outskirts of towns as occurs in agricultural areas of the south; and distribution of children of immigrants among all the schools in a district, avoiding the creation of "ghetto" schools.

The Catalan agricultural workers' union UP has set an example by providing contracts, documentation, housing and return air tickets for agricultural workers from Colombia and Morocco to pick fruit in Spain. The workers become part of the Social Security system and enjoy the protection of labour legislation and the chance to send their salary home. The union took this action when it was realised that 3,000 additional workers would be needed to help pick a bumper harvest. The programme has been copied by other groups such as the Association of Young Farmers of Almeria. However, some irregular workers already in Spain have complained that they had to return to their own countries in order to take advantage of the initiative.

Non-profit groups, however, are the main protagonists in Spanish society's efforts to welcome the newcomers. To give two examples from many: the Festival of World Music in Barcelona funded by the La Caixa Foundation gathered the city's immigrants together around the music of their respective countries; conferences and workshops on different cultures were subsequently held. In Malaga, the Aji-Atime association and other groups of immigrants organised a seminar on Youth and Immigration aiming to promote intercultural relations between young people of Spanish and Moroccan origin.

The importance of such actions should not be overestimated. More and more, younger and younger immigrants arrive in Spain, with an erroneous idea of a Europe where everything is straightforward and money is easy to obtain. But they arrive to find neither decent jobs nor security of residency to enable them to plan their lives, and there is a diffuse sense of rejection that is very threatening. Marginalisation and a crisis of identity contribute to violence, which itself feeds racism.

Sami Nair has pointed out that emphasising the identity of immigrants as a collective that differs from the host culture point for point, tends to reinforce prejudice[12]. History shows that migratory flows end in a common identity around shared values. Immigrants react as a group when they are marginalised on the basis of social position, language, and customs. Ideology of identity and ownership exists in order to provide a spiritual support to certain classes that have lost faith in the future. The danger is when questions of identity are articulated around prejudices and hide a hypocritical, seemingly inoffensive racism.

Abdelhamid Beyuki has said that the identities and cultures of each country are not set in stone, as racists think: "we are like this and they come from outside to dirty us."[13] To see immigrants solely as the solution to a problem of workforce and birthrate, so that they work, pay Social Security and then return home, is also to make a great mistake. In order to achieve a genuinely mixed society, as opposed to one formed of racial ghettos, he believes, Spain needs a policy of integration and interculturality based on living together, with programmes in schools, the streets and all areas of life.

Conclusions

In the past 25 years Spanish society has undergone many radical changes. One of these changes, most notably in the last decade, is the switch from being a nation of two million emigrants to a destination for hundreds of thousands of immigrants, some of whom find themselves starring on TV evening news bulletins when intercepted by the authorities.

It would be easy to blame this sudden, highly visible and unprecedented influx of would-be residents[14] for racist outbursts such as that of El Ejido, and for the institutional panic which caused the government to pass two major immigration laws —one liberal, one draconian— within the space of a year and twelve days. But while the sheer numbers of immigrants, their novelty and high media profile go some way to explain the reactions of certain sectors of Spanish society, they cannot be the whole story. In fact, Spain's treatment of its least favourite resident group, the gypsies, and the particular bias against

---

[12] "Inmigracion e identidad", *El País*, 12 March 2001.
[13] Interview, *Consumer* magazine, February 2001.
[14] As distinguished from tourists/pilgrims, who have contributed significantly to the Spanish economy for over a millennium.

immigrants from the Maghreb —both groups which have interacted extensively with Spaniards for hundreds of years— show that deeper and darker currents are at work. An unfamiliar face may provoke fear and mistrust; but one that you have learned, or been taught, to hate will generate far more dangerous emotions. Thus the widespread and generic problems experienced by immigrants from poorer countries to richer ones —which are common to many nations and many periods of history— may hide deeper and more specific evils which are very difficult to uproot.

In an era of economic liberalisation and uncontrolled trillion-dollar flows of capital at the speed of light (and with as little ethical conscience), it is inevitable that populations will migrate to follow capital investment, wherever it may go. It is equally inevitable that, whatever physical or legal barriers exist or are erected, a certain proportion of these migrants will succeed in getting to their destination. Given massive investment in a Martian colony, we would soon be seeing dangerously overloaded interplanetary pateras on the evening news.

In the absence of limitations on capital flow, it is up to individuals and institutions who have an interest in doing so, to protect the rights of the economic migrants who are bound to follow the money. This task falls mainly to NGOs, formed both by the immigrants themselves (their own states lacking the power to aid them) and by hospitable citizens of the host countries (whose governments, aside from any questions of institutional racism, are largely disinclined to help people who cannot vote).

The most serious acts of rejection of immigrants occurred in February, 2000, in the Almerian town of El Ejido, where the killing of a young woman by an immigrant unleashed an unprecedented wave of violence by the townspeople. The attacks were especially directed at the small minority of immigrants living in the city centre: those most integrated with the indigenous population. This was therefore a direct assault on cultural diversity in the city: an expression of fear that the immigrants should escape from the ghetto of exclusion to which they were confined.

The attitudes displayed in El Ejido fortunately are only a radical extreme of the opinions of Spanish people as a whole. Programmes of integration are being carried out by both governmental and non-governmental institutions. Ways of bringing illegal immigrants into the system are being studied, such as incrementing the quota agreements with countries of origin.

We might speak of immigrants as existing not just on the physical margins of the city, but also on the margins of citizenship (defined as a combination of rights, social duties and responsibilities, and social ties). Citizenship implies a relation between the citizen and the society as a whole, and participation in the construction of the collective and individual identity. Under current Spanish policy, documented immigrants are accorded the full rights of Spanish citizens as regards residence, legal process, etc.

With respect to forming public opinion, policies are needed that present the immigrant population as new citizens who join a society that is already diverse: policies which recognise the contribution made by immigrants to society and which respect the fundamental rights and freedoms of persons.

References

AJA, Eliseo. *La inmigración extranjera en España: los retos educativos.* Fundación La Caixa, Barcelona, 2000.
ALVITE, Juan Pedro; SUTCLIFFE, Bob. *Racismo, Antirracismo e Inmigración.* Gakoa Liburuak, Donostia, 1995, 1 Ed.
ARANGUEREN GONZALO, Luis A.; SAEZ ORTEGA, Pedro. *De la Toleracia a la Interculturalidad.* Anaya Ediciones, Madrid, 1998.
BACARIA, Jordi (Ed.), *Migración y Cooperación Mediterráneas.* Icaria Editorial, Barcelona, 1998.
BAUBÖCK, R. *Migration and Citizenship,* new Community 1991.
BLANCO FERNÁNDEZ DE VALDERRAMA, María Cristina. *Las migraciones contemporáneas.* Alianza, Madrid 1997.
CALVO BUEZAS, Tomas. *Inmigracion y Racismo.* Cauce, Madrid, 2000, 1 Ed.
CARRASCO CARPIO, Concepción. Colección Observatorio Permanente de la Inmigración. Mercados de Trabajo: *Los inmigrantes económicos.* Ministerio de Trabajo y Asuntos Sociales. 1999.
COLECTIVO IOÉ. Colección Observatorio Permanente de la Inmigración. *Inmigración y trabajo en España. Trabajadores inmigrantes en el sector de la hostelería.* Ministerio de Trabajo y Asuntos Sociales 1999.
DÍEZ NICOLÁS, Juan. Colección Observatorio Permanente de la Inmigración. *Los Españoles y la inmigración.* Ministerio de Trabajo y Asuntos Sociales. Octubre 1999.
GARCIA MARTINEZ, A.; SAEZ CARRERAS, J. *Del Racismo a la Interculturalidad.* Narcea Ediciones, Madrid, 1998.
GÓMEZ ALFARO, Antonio. *La gran redada de Gitanos.* Editorial Presencia Gitana. Colección Interface 1993.
GOYTISOLO, J.; NAIR, S.: *El peaje de la vida: integración o rechazo de la emigración en España.* Aguilar, Madrid, 2000.
IZQUIERDO ESCRIBANO, Antonio: *La inmigracion en España 1900-1990.* Ministerio de Trabajo y Seguridad Social, Madrid, 1992.

IZQUIERDO ESCRIBANO, Antonio: *La inmigración inesperada*, Trotta, Madrid. 1996.
JULIANO, Dolores. *Educacion Intercultural. Escuela y Minorias Etnicas.* Editorial Eudema, Madrid
KINCHELOE, Joe L.; STEINBERG, Shirley R. *Repensar El Multiculturalismo.* Ediciones Octaedro, Barcelona, 1999.
KORN, David A. *Exodus within borders: an introduction to the crisis of internal displacement.* Brooking Institution, Washington, 2000.
KOSLOWSKI, Rey. *Migrants and Citizens.* Cornell University Press, Ithaca, 2000.
KYMLICKA, Will. *Ciutadania Multicultural.* Edicions Proa, Barcelona, 1999.
LAMO DE ESPINOSA, Emilio (Ed.) *Culturas, Estados, Ciudadanos.* Alianza Editorial, Madrid, 1996, 1 Ed.
MAKOME, Inongo. *La Emigracion Negroafricana;* Carena, Barcelona, 2000.
MALGESINI, Graciela (Comp). *Cruzando Fronteras. Migraciones en el Sistema Mundial.* Icaria Editorial, Barcelona, 1998.
MALGESINI, Graciela; Gimenez, Carlos. *Guia de conceptos sobre Migraciones, Racismo e Interculturalidad.* Libros De La Catarata, Madrid, 2000.
MARTÍNEZ RODRIGO, Antonio. *España, país de inmigración: la condición de inmigrante.* Hoac, Madrid, 1992.
MARTÍNEZ VEIGA, Ubaldo. *El Ejido: discriminación, exclusión social y racismo.* Catarata, Madrid, 2001.
MARTINEZ VEIGA, Ubaldo. *La integración social de los inmigrantes Extranjeros en España.* 1997.
MARTINEZ VEIGA, Ubaldo. *Pobreza, segregación y exclusión espacial,* Icaria 1999.
MORERAS PALENZUELA, Jordi. *Musulmanes en Barcelona. Espacios y Dinamicas Comunitarias.* Fundacion Cidob, Barcelona.
NAIR, S.; LUCAS, J. de, Instituto de migraciones y servicios sociales. *El desplazamiento en el mundo: inmigración y tematicas de Identidad,* 1998.
NAZARET, M.; DE LA SOTA, T. (Coords.). Watu; *Diversidad Biologica, Diversidad Cultural.* Watu Accion Indigena, Madrid, 1997.
OLIVE, Leon. *Multiculturalismo y Pluralismo.* Editorial Paidos, Barcelona, 1999.
PAJARES, Miguel. *La inmigración en españa.* Icaria, Barcelona, 1998.
PANADERO MOYA, M.; GARCIA MARTINEZ, C. (Coords.). *Migraciones Extranjeras en la Union Europea.* Universidad de Castilla-La Mancha, Cuenca, 1997, 1 Ed.
PAPASTERGIADIS, Nikos. *The Turbulence of Migration.* Polity Press, Oxford, 1999.
Plan para la integración social de los inmigrantes. Ministerio de Asuntos Sociales. Dirección General de Migraciones 1994.
RIBAS MATEOS, Natalia. *Las Presencias de la Inmigracion Femenina.* Icaria Editorial, Barcelona, 1999, 1 Ed.
RUBIO-MARÍN, Ruth. *Immigration as a Democratic challenge citizenship and inclusion in Germany and the USA.* Cambrigde University Press 2000.
RUIZ OLABUENAGA, RUIZ VIEYTEZ, VICENTE TORRADO. *Los inmigrantes irregulares en España,* Universidad de Deusto, Bilbao 1999.
SOS RACISMO. *El Ejido: Racismo y explotación laboral.* Icaria, Barcelona 2001.

TODD, Emmanuel. *El Destino de los Inmigrantes.* Tusquets Editores, Barcelona, 1996, 1 Ed.
VERMEULEN, Hans; PERLMANN, Joel (Eds.). *Immigrants, Schooling and Social Mobility.* Macmillan, London, 2000.
WALLRAFF, Gunter. *Cabeza de Turco.* Editorial Anagrama, Barcelona, 1999.
WIEVIORKA, Michel. *El Espacio del Racismo.* Editorial Paidos, Barcelona.

When de-segregation produces stigmatisation: ethnic minorities and urban policies in France

Patrick Simon

Although France has been a land of immigration since the middle of the nineteenth century, for a long time the country did not adopt a definite doctrine explicitly describing the integration of foreigners. Such doctrine was rather inferred from the debate on the code of nationality (*code de la nationalité*) which gave rise to a definition of the "French individual" and of the conditions for assimilation. Fomal "rules", and the description of the means for incorporating foreigners into the body of the Nation over the last century and a half, only emerged at the beginning of the 1980s. An initial debate was launched by means of a "commission of wise men" established in 1987 by the Government in order to ease tensions raised by an attempted reform of the code of nationality. The work of the commission was published the following year (Commission de la nationalité, 1988). Later, in 1989, a new body was established, the High Council for Integration (Haut Conseil à l'Intégration) whose purpose was to inform and advise the authorities on immigrant integration. The Council soon announced that a voluntarist policy was on the agenda. Here is the most accurate institutional definition of the objective of any integration policy as devised by the HCI in 1991:

> Integration is a way to obtain the active participation in society as a whole of all women and men who are lastingly going to live on our land while overtly accepting that specific, mostly cultural, features will be preserved and nevertheless insisting on the similarities and the convergence, with equal rights and duties for all in order to preserve the cohesion of our social fabric. [...] Integration considers that differences are a part of a common project unlike either assimilation which aims at suppressing differences, or indeed insertion which establishes that their perpetuation is a guarantee for protection.[1]

---

[1] This is a revised and more accurate version of the definition presented in the first HCI report (HCI, 1993, p. 8).

While renewing the assimilationist tradition which is the essential feature of the French national model, the HCI struck a delicate balance between the rights and duties of "women and men who' are lastingly going to live on our land",[2] the acceptance of the basic values of the Republic, and the necessary transformation of French society in order to "leave some free space" for newcomers. This "integration model" sums up the long history of immigration and captures the essential principles of French integration policy in the making:

—Integration is an individual process which prohibits participation of immigrants in any structured communities whose institutionalisation poses a threat to the unity of the Nation;
—Admission as a citizen, i.e. becoming a French national, remains the pivot of the integration process. Maintaining an open code of nationality,[3] allowing for a rather sizeable admission of foreigners according to various procedures, ensures an ongoing "mixing" of populations. This is also a way of avoiding the emergence and perpetuation of "minorities" with specific legal statuses as a result of confusions between the notions of citizenship and nationality.
—The concept of integration is attached to the principle of equality in that it tries to practically reinforce the expression of equality in the social field.

According to this wording, the integration doctrine often clashes with practices, including institutional practices, which poorly reflect general principles. The firm opposition to the recognition of any structured communities which would add an intermediate stage between the authorities and individuals is often grossly disregarded in local compromises. The gap between tolerating specific cultural features and granting dispensations from the principles in the course of actual social interventions seems quite slim.[4] In terms of practical interventions,

---

[2] Note the use of the circumlocution which emphasises the lack of any appropriate term.

[3] The degree of "openness" of the code of nationality is debatable since the granting of nationality is partially a specific attribute of the State. Although there are few refusals, especially on grounds of "lack of assimilation", there is a reported increase in adjournments on grounds of job precariousness, which in turn has an aggravating effect on the economic instability of migrant populations. Adjournment criteria in cases of lack of professional activity were eased at the end of 1998, in order to better take into account all "insertion efforts made by applicants".

[4] Indeed the HCI are trying to strike a difficult balance when they acknowledge the legitimacy of active links and solidarities between people of a similar origin while

it is constantly being closed. In a way, the working out of French integration policies is a permanent quest to strike an unlikely —and even, according to many observers, unattainable— balance between an active tolerance of differences (including some concessions to the public expression of such differences) and the vigilant reassertion of the "principle of nondifferentiation".

When integration policies are carried out in practice, they mostly tend to facilitate the admission and settling in of immigrants while striving to incorporate them in the general legal framework. The fact that the administrative organisation of integration is distributed between various ministries (Ministry of Labour, Housing, Education, Justice, Home Office, Ministry of Urban Affairs, ...) testifies to the lack of clarification in the objectives of this policy, and in the end to a degree of helplessness in public intervention (VIET, 1998). This simply reflects the diversity of the fields which play a part in the process of "integration" and the practical difficulties in defining a "group" as a specific target. After painstakingly trying to derive policies from specific features and objectives while failing to define target groups (be they "foreigners", "excluded people", "discriminated against people") who do not fall into administrative classifications based on origin or race, integration policies later found an outlet through what we call "urban policy". Here, rather than naming populations, public action deals only with the territories (such as "neighbourhoods facing difficulties") where most problems to be tackled are concentrated. These territories are subjected to "affirmative action", which is a new notion by French standards and a rather hotly debated one too. Walking down this new road through the "neighbourhoods" makes it unnecessary to actually name the populations at whom special policies are directed. But this also means that in the end, the objective of making up for the damage suffered by those ethnic groups most discriminated against will be obscured by the struggle against segregation and the restoration of equality between the various territories.

With the rise of unemployment, labour relations no longer dominated our representation of society and the workplace was no longer the only setting for large-scale social conflicts. The workplace ceased to be the synthetic microcosm of social relationships; these were now played out in the neighbourhood. Tensions moved out into the open (DUBET/LAPEYRONNIE, 1992) and generally crystallised around a few symbols of social antagonism. In this context, the word

---

emphasising the danger of having "long lasting community gatherings", and even more so any institutional recognition of them.

"ghetto" became popular in reference to areas where rampant poverty and growing violence were a vivid proof of the demise of the French social model. Critics have often denounced the exaggerated use of this word, pointing out that it lacked precise definition and was often improperly used to describe situations having nothing to do with what, historically, came to be called "ghettos" (DE RUDDER, 1982; VIEILLARD-BARON, 1990; WACQUANT, 1992). Nevertheless, this vague concept now plays a central role in the symbolic management of social conflicts and underscores two strategic issues: 1) the recognition of ethnic diversity and of its impact both on social organisation and national symbolic representations; 2) the management of the territorialisation of social inequality, in other words the attempt to control a system whereby populations are confined to specific areas according to their socio-economic status or, which is even worse in a French perspective, to their position in the hierarchy of ethnic origins.

The concentration of immigrants in one area, as expressed in the both limited and highly emotional term "ghetto", is thus seen as symptomatic of the breakdown of the welfare state's social safety system, and as embodying the ongoing process of ethnic fragmentation.[5] Undermining, as they emerge, the foundations of the republican ideal of a Nation-State, these "ethnic enclaves" are perceived as the sign of the failure of integration, illustrating both its irrelevance as a model and the specificity of the behaviour of recently arrived immigrants. Furthermore, the outbreak of urban riots, with gangs of youths fighting the police against a setting of low-income housing projects, burning cars, looted supermakets and vandalised facilities, has shown to all that urban "marginality" breeds in a specific type of environment. Along the lines of the "social breakdown" (*fracture sociale*) theme, whereby people with low social status are "abandoned" and kept apart from the more successful groups (through processes of "disaffiliation" (CASTEL, 1995) or "disqualification" (PAUGAM, 1991), segregation is seen as the geographical illustration of the disintegration of social ties. The perception of social disorders as linked to specific areas has gained importance ever since the elaboration, in the early 1980s, of local social development policies under the cover-all label of "Urban Policy" (*Politique de la ville*). Spatial concentration and social disadvantage thus became increasingly linked. The idea that the concentration of "disqualified" populations was responsible for their social decline still prevails (PAUGAM, 1995).

---

[5] Concerning the responsibility of the welfare state in the "rise" of the ethnic phenomenon, see BJÖRKLUND, 1987.

The aim of this paper is not to verify or criticise the thesis of "neighbourhood impact" on the socio-economic situation or the status (in the Weberian sense of the word) of immigrants, but rather to identify the various mechanisms underlying these concentrations and discuss the problem of what they should be called —"ghetto", "ethnic neighbourhood", "integration area" (*quartier d'intégration*), "urban immigrant centre" (*espace de centralité immigrée*). The analysis of these processes and of their impact on immigrants' housing opportunities will be based on a dynamic view of these ethnic groups' itineraries rather than on a static description of their geographical distribution. This choice is warranted by the wish to understand how immigrants adjust their residential strategies to the obstacles set in their path by the housing market and public policies, obstacles which end up promoting an increasingly ethnically oriented segregation process. The role played by urban integration policies in the development and eradication of ethnic concentrations is ambiguous. Indeed, the filtering mechanisms set up to reduce the "ghettos" end up channelling households belonging to certain ethnic groups towards specific segments of the public housing stock, thus leading them to converge in the same area all over again. Deeper analysis of these policies and of their consequences on immigrants' residential itineraries should enable us to shed light on the French dilemma: how can ghettos be eliminated, or in other words, how can the ethnic distribution of the population be organised in such a way as to avoid the ethnic fragmentation of French society? Can this be achieved without having to elaborate policies specially targeted for immigrants, which would represent an unacceptable form of "multiculturalism" (WIEVORKA, 1996)?

Ethnicity and segregation: a question of concepts, methodology and sources

Statistics, by dividing society into normative categories, tend to maintain scientific investigation within the bounds of a predetermined framework. In the conflictual relationships between science and politics, statistics occupy a crucial position by their impact on the representation of society (DESROSIÈRES, 1993). This is all the more true of statistics describing immigrant or immigrant-related populations or dealing with ethnic diversity (PETERSEN, 1987).

For historical reasons, the categories used in French statistical analyses were, until recently, based on the legal definition of citizenship. No ethnic origin —or, since 1872, religious belief— could be used in describing the population of France. As a result, although sociologists were interested in "immigrants", statistics spoke only of "foreigners". This methodological twist made it difficult for researchers to analyse the dynamic of integration in France. Naturalisation, a procedure which is not overly difficult in France, has had a specific impact on the decrease in the foreign population: 1) since naturalisations usually occur after a long period of stay in the country, those who become French are usually in the later stages of their life; 2) there is a "generation trap door" resulting from the fact that, up to 1993, children born in France of foreign parents were automatically entitled to French citizenship at their legal majority; 3) naturalisation promotes "assimilation", which in official terms includes having a stable job, speaking French fluently and showing signs of loyalty towards one's adopted homeland. Naturalisation rates vary according to the country of origin. According to the 1990 census, 48 % of Spanish immigrants and 50 % of Italian immigrants had obtained French citizenship, compared to 13 % of Algerians, 15 % of Portuguese, 12 % of Moroccans and 10 % of Turks.

In 1990, statistical surveys on immigration began to refer to the category of "immigrant" to describe those who were born foreign citizens in a foreign country. By using this element as a main distinguishing factor, the impact of naturalisations on the population structure was neutralised, and interpretation errors in the evaluation of "the degree of integration of immigrants" avoided (TRIBALAT, 1989, 1991). In 1990, the population of France included 3.5 million foreign citizens and 4.2 million immigrants (7.4 % of the total population), a third of whom had become French citizens. The figures for the main immigrant communities present in France reflect the history of the different immigration waves since the beginning of the twentieth century. Thus, traces are left of the Polish wave of the 1920s and 1930s, and there are still many representatives of the Italian and Spanish waves (12 % and 10 %, respectively, of the total immigrant population in 1990). The waves of the 1960s are of course well represented, with 14 % Portuguese, 13 % Algerians, 11 % Moroccans. The more recent groups of immigrants are smaller, due to the stricter policies of immigration control implemented since 1974 and the early 1980s. The migratory flows from South-East Asia (4 %), Turkey (4 %) and French-speaking African countries (5 %) are gaining momentum, but given the present context, they probably will not reach the size of the previous waves (TRIBALAT, 1993).

However, the French category of "immigrant" does not correspond to that of "ethnic minority" in the US, Canada, or the UK (Statistics

Canada and US Bureau of the Census, 1993). French statistics refer to individuals in terms of nationality or place of birth, but make no mention of their origin, which is determined in other countries either by their parents' birthplace ("parentage nativity" in the US), or by a declaration of "ancestry" (US) or of "ethnic origin" (Canada and UK). The study of living conditions, economic situation or political participation of "ethnic minorities" remains deficient, since the concept does not actually mean anything. Children born of immigrants are not considered a statistical category, and descendants over several generations even less so. However, thanks to a simulation evaluating the "indirect input" of immigration, in other words the number of immigrants and immigrants' children and grandchildren in France since the beginning of the twentieth century, Tribalat was able to come up with the following results: "between 9.4 and 10.3 million people born in France and present in France on January 1st, 1986, — or in other terms between 19 % and 21 % of all persons born in France — have at least one immigrant parent or grandparent" (TRIBALAT, 1991, p. 24). If we look at the population of immigrants (*foreign born* in American terminology) and their children born in France (*native born from foreign born*), the entire group representing *foreign stock*, we have a figure of about 10 million, or 20 % of the population. For the purposes of comparison, in 1970, date of the last census for which these figures were available (LIEBERSON/WATERS, 1988), people of *foreign stock* represented 16.5 % of the population of the US. There is thus a striking contrast between the contribution of the immigrants to the French population and their incorporation in French symbolic representations. The situation is very different in the US, even though the demographic scale of immigration is comparable. These differences show that the two countries have, in fact, opposite "nation cultures".

These statistical constraints were reflected in the results of quantitative analyses. Studies on segregation ignored the dynamics of residential mobility and were unable to account for the emergence of immigrant groups which could not be strictly identified in terms of citizenship. The arrival of immigrants on the public scene paradoxically coincided with their disappearance from statistics. However, the specificity of the French approach is not limited to the negation of ethnic categories; it also concerns methodological choices. Synthetic indicators describing the distribution of social or ethnic groups in the city (dissimilarity, isolation, segregation) have only rarely been used to analyse segregation in France (BRUN, 1994), in contrast to America, where they are extensively, and sometimes excessively, referred to. There are no long-term statistical series concerning the history of segregation, which means that there is no data making it possible to analyse its various forms, especially in the case of immigrants. As a result, when ethnic concentrations began to be noticed and became the centre of public debates, such simple questions as these could not be answered: are concentrations of immigrant groups in specific neighbourhoods more frequent now than in the past? What causes these phenomena more commonly known as ghettos?

Studies on immigrants' residential movements have so far almost always been based on population censuses. Social geographers have studied this problem extensively and produced mapped analyses at the municipal or neighbourhood level (GUILLON, 1993). Furthermore, numerous local surveys have shown that immigrants usually occupy housing with the same specific and recurrent characteristics: either in public housing for those living in the periphery, or in old, rundown housing for those who live in the inner cities. Immigrants apparently tend to settle in the same types of urban environment (VILLANOVA/ BEKKAR, 1994). Until recently, other than geographical and administrative maps of immigrant residential distribution, the methods of factorial ecology had not been applied to this population (RHEIN, 1994). However, recent work by French researchers has made up for this deficiency.

The development of urban factorial ecology, in the context of "social area studies", has had a profound impact on the way social or ethnic segregation issues are approached. Data analysis methods have made it possible to tackle the question of why individuals choose either to live together or to avoid each other. Several studies have confirmed the typologies based on the analysis of correspondences (projection on a factorial plan) between residents' professions (TABARD, 1993), between profession and type of household (MANSUY/MARPSAT, 1991), and between housing stock characteristics and tenure statuses (SIMON, 1996a).

This article uses data from a survey on the living conditions of immigrants and their children (MGIS: *Mobilité Géographique et Insertion Sociale* - Geographical Mobility and Social Integration), carried out by INED in 1992 with a sample of 10,000 immigrants and 2,000 young people born in France of immigrant parents (TRIBALAT *et al.*, 1996). The survey focused on immigrants from several specific areas: Algeria, Morocco, Portugal, Spain, South-East Asia, sub-Saharan Africa and Turkey. The questionnaire inquired about the family, professional and residential histories of the respondents and included a number of questions concerning cultural, religious, linguistic and social practices (SIMON/TRIBALAT, 1993). Each respondent was linked to his/her residential block, itself identified and described thanks to a selection of variables taken from the 1990 census. Individual characteristics were thus considered in their local context. On the basis of the 6,544 blocks selected for the survey, a typology of residential contexts was elaborated thanks to the combination of a factorial analysis and an upward hierarchical classification ("*Classification par ascendance hiérarchique*") of housing stock characteristics and occupancy types (SIMON, 1996a). The results are thus not representative of the entire country, but only of the location of each sample group. Unless otherwise specified, the figures quoted hereafter are taken from the census or the MGIS survey.

A brief history of immigration and of immigrants' residential itineraries in France

The main waves of immigrants arriving in the 1920s and 1930s usually settled near large mining fields (ore, coal) and industrial plants (chemical, iron and steel industries), or in agricultural regions. Contrary to what is most commonly thought, they did not disperse to other parts of the country any faster or more easily in the twenties than they do now. In fact, employers encouraged migrants to remain in the same area, together with their families and countrymen (NOIRIEL, 1989). Italian, Polish, Spanish neighbourhoods, and sometimes even entire villages, were thus created (LEQUIN, 1988). In the 1926 census, many municipalities had a very high proportion of immigrants among their residents, as pointed out in the study published by G. Mauco in 1932:

> in the town of Joeuf-Homécourt, in the region of Meurthe-et-Moselle, there are 8,200 Italians and 2,800 Poles for a total population of 17,000; in the town of Villerupt, where 3/4 of the population is foreign, one has the impression of being in Italy. [...] The same can be said for regions where new electro-metallurgical and chemical industries are developing. In Villard-Bonnot, in the Isère region, out of a population of 5,442, there are 5,300 foreign residents, a proportion of 95%! [...] Foreign enclaves also exist in the countryside, in the South-West, in Normandy and in the North. The village of Villeneuve in the Haute-Marne region is Dutch, Blanquefort in the Gers is Italian, and so few Frenchmen live there that it is difficult to find members for the municipal council or to appoint a mayor (Mauco, 1932, p.138).

Until the end of the 1930s, the main immigrant communities gradually made their way into French society, while at the same time creating specific structures and institutions to meet the needs of their group. Large communities of Spanish, Italian (MILZA, 1986), Polish (PONTY, 1988), Armenian (HOVANESSIAN, 1992), and other immigrants thus lived and grew in a context marked by a rather complex infrastructure of shops, schools, places of worship, and by the emergence of community leaders. Not only were these groups located in geographically circumscribed areas, but they also tended to specialise in certain professions. Thus, in 1930, in the departments of Alpes-Maritimes, Var and Bouches-du-Rhône, 75 % of construction workers and 62 % of unskilled workers, dockers and packers were Italian. Evidence shows that the development of "immigrant neighbourhoods" dates back to the very first mass migrations. The same phenomenon occurred at the time of migrations from the provinces to the city: migrants from the same region would temporarily settle together, near one of the main gates of a large city, and then gradually disperse. Several "provincial" colonies have nevertheless survived, with their own self-help groups, cafés and shops, and even parish churches frequented by the "*pays*" (people who come from the same village or locality) (CHEVALIER, 1950).

In the early 1950s, new groups of immigrants began to arrive in France. From 2 million in 1946, they totalled 3.4 million in 1968. When Algeria became a French department in 1946, exchanges between the two territories increased. Along with Algerian-born immigrants, migrants from Italy and Spain began to pour in; to these waves, one must add the influx of Portuguese workers at the end of the 1960s. The Portuguese wave, although short-lived (barely ten years), involved a very large number of people, with 50,000 immigrants in 1962 and 759,000 in 1968. Finally, the exodus of the "boat people" from former Indochina brought over 100,000 people within a few years. At the same time, immigrants began to come in from other North African countries and the former French colonies in Africa, as well as Turkey and the Indian Subcontinent.

Urban housing infrastructures were unable to provide enough decent housing for this massive influx of migrant workers, whose families often subsequently came to join them. Since public authorities were also unable to meet the urgent housing needs of these new immigrants, the latter had no choice but to settle in abandoned or insalubrious housing; shantytowns sprouted in the outskirts of Paris, Lyons, Grenoble and Marseilles, providing shelter for those who were excluded from the "slum market" (BACHMANN/LEGUENNEC, 1996; VOLOVITCH-TAVARES, 1995). Public authorities then decided to get rid of the slums and set up specific housing structures for "foreign workers". An organisation called SONACOTRA was created in 1956 to manage special hostels, at first only for Algerian workers, and from 1963 on, for all foreign workers. At the same time, an interministerial group (GIP) was entrusted with the task of eliminating the shantytowns and inner-city slums. In 1975, part (20 %) of the "1 % for housing" tax was allocated to immigrant housing. In 1981, this proportion was reduced to 6.4 %. These funds, however, were never exclusively devoted to the construction of public housing for foreigners (WEIL, 1991).

Most immigrants arriving in the 1960s lived in substandard housing. Over 35 % of the immigrants from Algeria, Morocco or sub-Saharan Africa lived precariously, in hostel rooms, furnished tenements and shanties, and this proportion rose to 55 % for those who came without their families. Those whose families came to live in France rarely remained in "precarious" housing. In 1974, the country's 680 hostels housed 170,000 foreigners. Today, about 100,000 immigrants live in this type of accommodation, most of whom come from North Africa (63 %) and sub-Saharan Africa (22 %) (BERNARDOT, 1995). With the implementation in the 1970s of programmes to eliminate the slums, many migrant families living in shantytowns were transferred to the "*cités de transit*" (transitional housing projects). These forms of accommodation were meant for households who had left the slums or for newly-arrived immigrants; they were intended as "transitional dwellings", enabling households to "adapt" before moving to conventional public housing. In practice, the families often ended up staying indefinitely in these supposedly transitional dwellings.

Between 1975 and 1990, the proportion of foreign households living in precarious housing fell from 10 % to 4 %. Algerians were relatively quick to leave the furnished tenements: within 15 years, 70 % of households had moved to other types of housing, especially public housing. Housing without basic amenities now represents only 15 % of immigrants' dwellings, as opposed to 48 % in 1975. The living conditions of immigrants improved thanks to two main factors: "upward" residential mobility, and the destruction of insalubrious inner-city slums, more commonly known as "*de facto* social housing stock". Since the 1960s, 85 % of the furnished tenements have been demolished, and between 1975 and 1990, so was 70 % of the pre-1949 urban housing stock without amenities. The structural modifications of the housing stock thus paralleled, and even magnified immigrants' patterns of residential movement.

As immigrants gradually moved to conventional housing, they settled to a large extent in the public sector, while those who had previously lived there moved up in the housing hierarchy. For the most part, public housing built in the 1960s had not aged well. Furthermore, middle class French households took advantage of the last years of inflation to invest in property and move out of their public housing apartments. Thanks to these new vacancies, the more disfavoured families were able to move in (TANTER/TOUBON, 1995). At the end of the 1970s and in the early 1980s, the HLM companies (*Habitat à Loyer Modéré* —public social housing) changed their policy and began to grant housing to families which had been turned out of the inner cities, then under renovation[6]. The vacancies were thus occupied by immigrant families in need of larger apartments. The massive arrival of immigrants, however, discredited the social housing sector and triggered a downward spiral of social stigma, physical degradation and segregation. Indeed, immigrants usually lived in the least attractive sectors of the social housing stock. As their presence in an area became a clear sign of the latter's loss of prestige, their numbers declined in the neighbourhoods targeted by urban renewal projects (gentrification of the city centre). As a result, from the mid-seventies on, the rate of concentration of immigrants rose sharply in the most deteriorated segments of the social housing stock.

Nevertheless, not all immigrants choose to live in public housing. Although almost 50 % of North Africans and Turks live in HLM apartments, this is true of only 25 % of the Portuguese and 18 % of the Spanish immigrants (see table 1). An analysis of immigrants' residential movements after their arrival in France shows two distinct patterns (SIMON, 1996b). The first, which we will call the "entrepreneurial model", is based on a very dynamic owner-occupation strategy. The households in this category remain in control of their decisions and choices and manage to stay out of both the state or public housing allocation systems and out of private rental housing. This is typical of Portuguese, Spanish or Asian immigrants and goes along with the development of an ethnic business sector, either trade or small sub-contracting firms in the construction or electronics industries (MA MUNG, 1994). The second group of immigrants improve their housing conditions not by becoming owners but by obtaining an apartment in social housing projects. Since the housing allocation system is strictly controlled, households have little freedom of choice and their dependence on the state increases. This is most often the case for North African and Turkish immigrants. This residential choice is linked to the nature of their professions: they are often salaried industrial workers and as such particularly vulnerable to streamlining. Indeed, the unemployment rate reaches 26-29 % for men and 36-44 % for women, as compared to an

---

[6] In 1973, 12% of the households living in HLM housing belonged to the lowest income quartile, whereas this proportion rose to 32% in 1992.

average of 19 % and 22 %, respectively, for the entire French population (INSEE, 1997, p. 85). Due to their precarious economic situation, these groups are increasingly dependent on the social welfare system.

The ethnicisation of social segregation

The high degree of hierarchisation between different residential areas is the first sign of unequal social distribution within the urban space. When households move from one area to the other of this segregated space, they either modify or reinforce the social division of the city. At the same time, in a segregated system, residential moves depend on the concerned household's financial situation and "social reputation". French cities were shaped by social hierarchy, in terms of profession, income, and family structures (MANSUY/MARPSAT, 1991), and this remains true of most European cities (KNOX, 1995). A. Chenu and N. Tabard have pointed out that from 1982 to 1990, the division of urban space into socio-economically marked areas has intensified. Here are the main trends observed:

— the gentrification of well-to-do areas. Upper level professionals, company directors, and liberal professionals tend to settle in areas where their professions are well represented (gentrification by aggregation); in other cases, the gentrification process occurs when the lower classes are evicted (gentrification through exclusion);
— "technical" professions settle in working class and artisan areas, and correlatively, the service sector expands in the areas where technical professions dominate (CHENU/TABARD, 1993).

These observations have been more recently confirmed and completed by a study carried out by P. Bessy and N. Tabard. This analysis, which looks at the residential mobility of households between 1982 and 1990, shows the crucial role played by residential mobility in the social standing of an area (BESSY/TABARD, 1996).

This is the difficult context faced by immigrant families wishing to improve their living conditions. Indeed, immigrants occupy a rather specific place in professional stratification. Globally speaking, they are over-represented in low-skilled jobs and in independent professions (GUILLON, 1996). At the local level, the degree of over-representation can be quite high, since immigrants tend to be identified with a given socio-professional group. In the working-class neighbourhood of Belleville, in Paris, immigrants represent 28.5 % of the working population, but

62 % of the unskilled workers and 45 % of unemployed. In the blocks with the highest concentrations of immigrants, the latter represent 40 % of the population, 81 % of unskilled workers and 71 % of unemployed (SIMON, 1995). To complete the picture, we may look at incomes: the first decile of average incomes in France is about 90,000 francs per year. This amount is earned by 13 % of Spanish, Portuguese and South-East Asian immigrants, 20 % of Algerian immigrants, 24 % of Africans and 27 % of Turkish immigrants. Between 89 % and 77 % of Turkish, North African and African households earn less than the French median income (INSEE, 1997:100).

In addition to socio-economic constraints, immigrants must face discrimination based on their ethnic origin or race. This type of discrimination has not been studied much in France. It involves refusals to rent dwellings and filtering processes for access to certain types of housing; as a result, the most stigmatised groups are oriented towards specific sectors of the housing stock. These various and contrasting processes have led to the intensification of immigrant concentration in several parts of large urban agglomerations (DESPLANQUES/TABARD, 1991). According to G. Desplanques and N. Tabard, the analysis of professional positions shows a phenomenon of "overconcentration" of immigrants. The concentration of Algerians, Moroccans, Tunisians and Africans in "poor working-class" neighbourhoods is higher than that of French citizens with the same level of professional qualification. On the other hand, Portuguese, Spanish and Italian immigrants are not concerned in this process.

The diversity of immigrants' residential contexts is shown in the distribution of immigrants of different origins according to housing types (table 2). Portuguese and Spanish immigrants tend to live in detached houses, Turks, Algerians and Moroccans tend to settle in public housing projects, and South-East Asians often live in recently-built apartment buildings, either in the inner city or in the suburbs. Last, African immigrants tend to cluster in the old central neighbourhoods and in renovated or recently-built areas, living in disused apartment buildings which have not yet been renovated. Developers of low quality, hard-to-sell plots of land set up contacts with African community leaders. These channel African households which are unable to find public or private rental housing towards these owner-occupation programmes (POIRET, 1996). As a result, the social standing of an area is in accordance with the social imprint of a given type of housing. Turkish, Moroccan and Algerian immigrants tend to live in working-class neighbourhoods, whereas Portuguese and Spanish migrants live in middle-class neighbourhoods; the proportion of South-East Asians and

African immigrants is higher than average in the upper middle-class and well-to-do neighbourhoods.

The analysis of social dissimilarity indexes, which measure the difference in the relative share of socio-professional categories between immigrant and "native" groups, shows a mix between the social position and ethnic origin (table 3). The areas with the lowest indices are those where filtering processes are most active, due to allocation policies in the case of public housing, or economic selection or coopting for detached housing areas. However, the similarities between the social profiles of immigrant and "native" residents tend to decrease as the proportion of immigrants rises. Thus, in neighbourhoods with lower concentrations of immigrants, the proportion of blue-collar workers among the "natives" is 37%, and rises to 48% in neighbourhoods with high levels of immigrant concentration; within the immigrant community, the increase grows sharper, from 54% to 75%. This situation reflects the slowing down of the upward residential mobility process in the more deteriorated sectors of the housing stock. Having left the slums for normal housing, working class immigrants move in next door to native households, which for their part have not moved up in the housing hierarchy. Another sign of the difference in the social status of these two types of populations is the higher rate of unemployment among immigrants, since they are 1.5 times more prone to joblessness than "natives". Thus, even in neighbourhoods where housing allocation policies aim to reduce social disparities, immigrants remain in a position of inferiority.

The social disparity indices registered in social housing neighbourhoods are nevertheless much lower than those of cosmopolitan neighbourhoods. In these areas, there is a wide gap between immigrants working at rather poorly qualified jobs or in small food or repair shops and native inhabitants whose professional positions are middle or upper level. In these conditions, social diversity goes along with a greater inequality of social statuses, and this can also be seen in the difference in unemployment rates. Although the ratio of over-representation[7] of unskilled and skilled immigrant workers is about 125 in social housing neighbourhoods, it reaches 180 in city centres. The social division of urban centres is thus increasingly based on ethnic criteria. Native blue-collar workers have moved out of these areas and are replaced by recently arrived immigrants. In these urban contexts, the congruence between social class and ethnic origin is reinforced.

---

[7] Over-representation is calculated as the ratio of the % of immigrants among unskilled and skilled workers to the % of immigrants in the total working population.

The proportion of immigrants increases as the scale becomes smaller, from municipality to neighbourhood to block. At the local level, some spots reach very high degrees of concentration, for instance in suburban housing projects outside Paris, Lyons, Marseilles, Grenoble. Neighbourhoods where 50 to 60 % of the population is of immigrant origin are not infrequent. However, neighbourhoods with only one ethnic group are very rare. Usually, many different origins are represented, and in that sense, this form of segregation differs from the mono-ethnic "ghetto" type (VIEILLARD-BARON, 1994).

Ethnic neighbourhoods

When the most stigmatised ethnic groups moved to conventional housing and especially to the deteriorated social housing projects, immigrants all of a sudden became much more noticeable. However, this heightened perception of ethnic segregation occurred precisely at the time when the rate of concentration of immigrants in certain types of housing (workers' hostels, furnished tenements, insalubrious buildings) was in fact decreasing. The seventies saw the beginning of a process which may be called, using Habermas' terminology, the *publicisation* of immigrant populations: leaving their areas of confinement, they gradually made their way into mainstream society (DE RUDDER, 1993). Immigrants began to play a major role, on the job market, the housing market, in schools, to such an extent that part of the French population began to voice dissatisfaction about their presence and even reject them. The conflicts which then broke out, owing either to difficult neighbourhood relationships or competition over increasingly scarce jobs, were the direct consequence of the "cohabitation" of native and immigrant populations in residential areas and the decompartmentalisation of the job market. Since immigrants and native French citizens were increasingly in contact, or "competing", as urban ecology terms it, conflicts over the issue of "legitimate rights" arose, which in their most acute expression took the form of demands for "national preference"; most of the time, however, they were expressed in the form of antagonistic behaviour and a refusal to accept the idea of "difference" embodied by immigrants. Ethnic tensions emerged as a consequence of the desegregation process initiated in the late sixties.

These neighbourhood conflicts, which have already been analysed in the conceptual framework of "racial relationship cycles" as applied to the question of residential succession (DUNCAN/DUNCAN, 1965), are a sign that a specific process of appropriation is under way in areas of high immigrant concentration, resulting in the emergence of "ethnic neighbourhoods". This process linking an ethnic group to a specific "territory", and called "territorialisation", has been observed in most areas with large immigrant communities (BATTEGAY, 1992). As shown in the Chicago school models, "territorialisation" is a stage in the long process of assimilation of immigrants into mainstream society. Immigrant neighbourhoods are considered transitional, or, as E. Burgess put it, they are "first entry ports", making it easier for immigrants to bear separation from home and gradually integrate into mainstream society (BURGESS, 1925). This is why immigrants often recreate their original surroundings in these neighbourhoods: ethnic shops selling native foods and other products, community groups and associations helping people out with bureaucracy and providing them with the information needed to get by in their new environment (reading and writing skills, knowledge of social rights, family planning, learning to use the health care services, etc.). By maintaining a balance between their past and new environments, these various structures play an important role in helping immigrants adapt to their new society.

Immigrant neighbourhoods also play a crucial role in the development of community structures. The grouping of a specific population together with the development of what R. BRETON (1964) has called "institutional completeness" are what holds ethnic communities or "quasi-communities" together, according to H.J. Gans (GANS, 1962). J. Remy has suggested calling these areas, where one or several ethnic communities have established their networks of relations and structures, "founding neighbourhoods" (REMY, 1990). We suggest using the term "integration neighbourhoods", to underscore the role played by local community facilities, created by and for the community, in the process of integration of immigrants into the city and eventually into mainstream society[8] (SIMON, 1992). True, the fact that this form of social organisation coincides with a circumscribed area is reminiscent of the ghetto. However, several important differences should be pointed out:

— ethnic neighbourhoods do not owe their existence to an arbitrary political decision, but to an ordinary though powerful combination of socio-economic segregation and ethnic-racial discrimination.

---

[8] It should be pointed out here that integration into the city does not necessarily entail integration into the nation, since these two entities, city and nation, have different sets of values and norms which operate at different levels.

— the inhabitants of "ethnic neighbourhoods" in "post-modern" or "global" cities do not necessarily carry out all their activities in one location. Because of zoning, people constantly travel from area to area, for work, school, leisure or shopping. This everyday mobility tempers the "total" nature of the ghetto as formulated by Wirth. Indeed, the residents of even the most closed-in neighbourhoods, those who bear the worst stigma because of where they live, always have access to the rest of the city and other more distant areas. Thus, the identification between neighbourhood and community must be seen in a more dynamic fashion: space is no longer the main organising factor, it is an element which structures community relations and is to be ultimately overcome, and even subverted (WELLMAN/LEIGHTON, 1981). The notion of "ethnic enclave" has given rise to numerous debates (WILSON/PORTES, 1980; SANDERS/NEE, 1987, 1992; PORTES/JENSEN, 1987, 1989, 1992; WALDINGER, 1996) which have underscored the ambiguity of the notion of territorial enclave taken in the strictly geographical sense of the word, as opposed to the more immaterial concept of economic or social "niche".

— there is a considerable difference between the white immigrant "ethnic neighbourhoods" of American cities and the black ghettos, where population density, along with social troubles and violence, are much greater than in white ethnic neighbourhoods. P. Jargowsky distinguishes several forms of "neighbourhood poverty": the predominantly black ghettos, the predominantly Hispanic *barrios*, the predominantly white, non-Hispanic "White slums" and the mixed slums, which are not dominated by any specific race or ethnic group (JARGOWSKY, 1996:14). These forms of ethnic or racial concentration have no equivalents in French cities. Even though some neighbourhoods are sometimes called "Arab medinas", "Chinatown" or Central and Eastern European Jewish "Pletzl", these names refer to the fact that these communities, even though they may not represent the majority of the local population, have taken over the neighbourhood's public and commercial space.

Recent studies carried out in France on "ethnic neighbourhoods" show that ethnic groups often do not live the areas where they socialise. The function of ethnic neighbourhoods, which at first was to welcome recently arrived immigrants, is now changing, and this transformation was accelerated by the increasing restrictions on immigration implemented since 1974. Researchers now describe them as "*espaces de centralité immigrée* (central immigrant areas)" (TOUBON/MESSAMAH, 1991). The notion of centre no longer refers to population concentration in terms of numbers, but to the economic, cultural and social specialisation of a given area: the latter is a centre of attraction for an ethnic community whose members, though living elsewhere, often come to shop or socialise. Even though high residential density is not a prerequisite for the emergence of these new functions, nevertheless, it is supported by the presence of ethnic groups in the area. Indeed, a community's activities are what determines a neighbourhood's character and image, and up to a certain point, they play a role in determining the profile of the local residents.

The notion of "centrality" can perfectly well refer to a system of residential dispersion combined with the grouping of activities, as noted by A. Raulin in her study of Paris' Little Asia —the Choisy neighbourhood in the 13th arrondissement. Though the Asian community has taken over most of the commercial space available in this neighbourhood, the proportion of Asian residents is decreasing. According to the author, there is a "territorial separation between residential and commercial areas". She continues: "Ethnic or cultural communities living in today's urban (or posturban) context do not necessarily mark their presence by taking over an area for the purposes of residing, shopping, working and religious worship all at once. Not only do these different functions tend to be located in different areas, but immigrant communities are less and less likely to systematically use territory as a strategy; instead, they create 'social networks' which can overcome distance thanks to modern communication and transport technologies" (RAULIN, 1988, p. 240). This new type of centrality is not in contradiction with the notion of "transitional area", even though it represents another stage in the settling down process. Indeed, it is an extension of the "transitional area" phase and should disappear once the integration process is completed, at which point "centrality", as a function, should ultimately lose its reason for existence. These new forms of "consumption at a distance" are in keeping with the traditional practices of diasporas such as the South-East Asian and Jewish diasporas. For the other groups, ethnic commercial and cultural centres were seldom able to exist without the support of a local resident community.

However, other than these symbolically marked neighbourhoods, most suburban immigrant concentrations have been unable to develop specific community structures. Shopping areas are weakly developed, and despite efforts, community groups and associations have difficulty livening up the dreary atmosphere of these desolate areas. This anomic world of "housing projects" is home to a bored younger generation, whose idleness is perceived by other residents as potentially threatening. These "projects" have neither social order, nor history, nor memory; everyday life is under constant tension, with people living in an atmosphere of small-time crime and delinquency, drug addiction and dealing, degraded living conditions, in a world of joblessness, inaction and poverty. In this context appeared the first signs of an oncoming urban crisis, which would eventually lead to a complete review of the state's role in the regulation of social problems.

Public policies and the ghetto dilemma

In the 1980s, scenes of urban rioting brutally revealed that a serious crisis was brewing in many social housing neighbourhoods. Several reports warned public authorities about the urgency of the problem. In the most famous of these reports, the author, H. Dubedout, drew the outline of the future "*Politique de la Ville* (Urban Policy)". Describing the emotion felt by the public after the riots, he wrote: "The media were broadcasting to a surprised and concerned nation the image of ghettos where people and families rejected by the rest of the city and society, lived in a uniform, deteriorated and soulless environment. [...] The public found out about such neighbourhoods as 'les Minguettes' in the city of Vénissieux, those of northern Marseilles, the slums of Roubaix, the 'Haut du Lièvre' housing project in Nancy, the 'cité des 4000' in La Courneuve" (DUBEDOUT, 1983, p. 5). The situation was indeed problematic, owing to a combination of negative factors: the state of deterioration of many public housing projects, the "cohabitation" of populations whose histories and social behaviour differed, the economic decline of neighbouring sources of employment, the arrival on a depressed job market of a large group of poorly qualified young people. Given the role played by young people of immigrant origin in suburban social unrest, the public's awareness of this ethnic mosaic increased. The sight of these areas inhabited by poor and immigrant households evicted from renewed city centres brought to mind frightening images of ethnic or social "ghettos". It also rekindled old fears of crime-ridden and dangerous working class suburbs (CHEVALIER, 1958).

Following the example of the cities, employment policies also went through a crisis. With growing joblessness and an increasing discrepancy between people's level of training and qualification and the needs of the job market, it became clear that the existing system had to be changed. A new approach linking socio-professional qualification to social integration was worked out. Access to the employment market could only be ensured once a person was successfully integrated into the local environment. This new locally based employment policy was developed in the framework of the decentralisation of public action, according to which social and economic decisions are made on a regional basis (WUHL, 1996). This new focus on local action led to the creation of a special programme, called "Neighbourhood Social Development" (*Développement Social des Quartiers*, DSQ), aimed at revitalising the economic and social environment of these neighbourhoods while helping "disqualified" persons regain their status in society.

Politically, segregation has became intolerable in a democratic state whose founding principles include the equality of all citizens. There is thus a wide consensus on the necessity of eradicating it. However, the term "segregation" refers to a wide variety of situations and processes, and as a result, many possible forms of intervention exist, which at times may even be contradictory (DAMAMME/JOBERT, 1995). With the Urban Policy, the aim of public authorities is to fight social exclusion by working on its spatial expression: the priority objectives of public action are to pull disfavoured neighbourhoods out of their isolation, revitalise these desolate areas, and patch up the breakdown in social ties. Though this Urban Policy was launched in 1977 through the Housing and Social Life (*Habitat et Vie Sociale*) programme, which concerned several pilot neighbourhoods, it actually only became operational in 1982. The initial intent of the DSQ programme was first and foremost to avoid dividing public and community action into various compartments, such as social aid, schools, housing, health care, etc. As Donzelot and Estèbe describe it, the role of the state should be that of an organiser ("*Etat-animateur*"), coordinating all the different actors in charge of implementing the Urban Policy (DONZELOT/ESTÈBE, 1994).

The Urban Policy concerns a selection of "priority" neighbourhoods, termed "problem neighbourhoods (*quartiers en difficulté*)", or "neighbourhoods at risk (*quartiers à risque*)", or "sensitive areas (*zones sensibles*)", etc. With each programme, the list of selected neighbourhoods lengthened: 148 in 1982, over 500 with the 10th plan in 1989, and finally, with the "city contracts" (*contrats de ville*) of the 11th plan, the figure rose to 1500. Several methodical studies on these "priority" neighbourhoods have been carried out (CHAMPION/GOLDBERGER/ MARPSAT, 1992; TABARD, 1993; CHAMPION/MARPSAT, 1996) and have shown that these selections were not sociologically coherent. According to N. Tabard, "although the neighbourhoods targeted by the Urban Policy do not rank very high in the socio-spatial hierarchy

[...], their situation is nevertheless not the worst, neither within their own city, nor as compared to other cities" (TABARD, 1993:16). The composition of the selected neighbourhoods is extremely varied (in terms of household types, unemployment rates, professions, proportion of young people under age 20, proportion of foreigners), thus revealing both a great diversity of situations and the lack of coherence in the choices made.

The DSQ programme is not the only existing territorial approach to social problems. Other forms of state intervention have been devised, such as the ZEP status (*Zone d'Education Prioritaire* - Priority Education Area), granted to approximately 600 areas in France, each often covering several school establishments; the CCPD (*Conseils Communaux de Prévention de la Délinquance* - Municipal Council for the Prevention of Delinquency, 735 in 1993), or the *missions locales pour l'insertion des jeunes en difficulté* (local missions for the social integration of disadvantaged young people —221 offices). Public intervention thus heavily relies on local forms of action, as shown by these decentralised programmes. However, this emphasis on the local nature of public action reinforces the spatial factor and underscores the link between social exclusion and geographical exile. Thus, the new role played by local authorities as purveyors of public action is one of the most striking aspects in the redefinition of the "social issue". Disfavoured neighbourhoods receive special funding, but they are at the same time stigmatised. The linking of social problems to a specific area thus fosters a vicious circle: the neighbourhood's reputation is tarnished by the fact that its residents are poor, and the residents are in turn socially stigmatised for living in a "bad" neighbourhood. In addition to having to deal with concrete problems, the neighbourhood is branded with a negative image; as a result, both the neighbourhood and its inhabitants end up falling deeper into a downward spiral of depreciation.

The problem of segregation became the focus of urban policies with the implementation of the July 1991 Orientation Law for the City (*Loi d'Orientation pour la Ville*, LOV).[9] The aim of this law was to promote *diversity* in cities, in terms both of housing and population. In

---

[9] The first chapter of the Orientation Law for the City begins: "So that urban residents may enjoy the right to live decently in the city, the municipalities (etc.) must provide them with the living and housing conditions necessary in order to maintain social cohesion, and *avoid or eliminate segregation*. The aim of this policy is to ensure the integration of each neighbourhood into the city and the *coexistence of different social categories in every urban agglomeration*" (*Journal Officiel*, 19 July 1991, emphasis added).

this sense, the LOV established an implicit connection between social harmony and the coexistence of different populations and types of housing. Public policies, having renewed the ideal vision of a city inhabited by a mix of social groups living together and, thanks to this proximity, interacting more or less closely, were once again trying to "organise society through urban reform" (TOPALOV, 1991, p. 61). However, the context in which the "social mix" myth was being revived had changed. In the past, the role of public action had consisted in eradicating insalubrious housing and providing their former residents with "adequate" housing. Since the working classes had been kept in the slums by greedy speculators and property-owners eager to make as much profit as they could, it was up to the state to intervene as a market regulator, and later on as a manager, and provide decent housing to the working classes. The latter were thus "concentrated" in social housing areas, the main targets of public action. But the decline of these "large social housing projects" (*grands ensembles*) revealed a fundamental contradiction in the state's system of action: the Urban Policy was trying to reform what was already the result of reform. In this context, the welfare state found itself in a quandary: since state intervention had a minor impact on the segregational processes caused by city life itself, what was to be done?

The LOV tried to counter this determinism by encouraging well-to-do households to move to working class neighbourhoods, and creating ways for "disfavoured" households to move to better neighbourhoods. Nevertheless, the rationale followed by the LOV still remained one of strict control over where the working classes lived. The aim was thus not to grant freedom of residential choice to the victims of segregation —or at least those so considered— but to create a social and ethnic patchwork by arbitrarily dispersing them throughout the city. However, planning the ethnic and social composition of an area meant *de facto* dismantling the relationship networks based on the social or ethnic homogeneity of working class neighbourhoods. The policy of spreading disfavoured populations throughout the city was specifically intended as a means of countering the concentration of immigrants in one area. The Urban Policy's avowed aim was "to fight exclusion by refusing to accept a two-tiered society" (GEINDRE, 1993, preface), but at the same time, analysts of the urban crisis link the growing unemployment rate among immigrants to their increasingly autonomous lifestyle:

> In some neighbourhoods, the laws of the republic are increasingly losing hold. The problems of ethnic "cohabitation" must not be ignored: what is considered in France "relative poverty" represents a

much higher standard of living than that of most inhabitants of the Third World, and for that reason, cities will continue to attract immigrants. But if the immigrants who arrived in France during the thirty "glorious" postwar years (les Trentes Glorieuses) had a good chance of integrating into French society, what about the immigrants or children of immigrants who are now unemployed? Just as in the United States and in Great Britain, those who live in disfavoured neighbourhoods have begun to search for an identity as members of an ethnic community, and one may reasonably see this trend as a potential threat to the non-religious principles and values of the French republic (Geindre, 1993, preface).

Although the situation of immigrants has been identified as a significant factor in the urban crisis, surprisingly enough this fact is ignored by major public policy directives. Public authorities have always understood the strategic nature of the issue of the social integration of immigrants, even to the extent that a ministry was set up for that purpose, but nonetheless, no policy ever addressed the specific problems of immigrants (CHEBBAH, 1996). In contrast with this absence of policy, immigrants must withstand a double accusation: on one hand, they are considered potential trouble-makers and on the other, they are a visible and unwelcome proof of the existence of social inequalities, of which they themselves are the first victims. But state action directed to a specific area would be considered a form of positive discrimination, which the "French model of integration" does not accept. Thus, the development of locally oriented public action can be seen as an attempt to adapt common-law policies to specific situations. The ZEP programmes can thus be justified, since their aim is to deal with the educational problems of the children of immigrants, using intercultural pedagogical methods (LORCERIE, 1995). This type of action, however, contradicts the principle of not differentiating ethnic origins and providing the same type of education to all, regardless of the district. Nevertheless, such deviations from the national norm and republican principles are tolerated in areas of high immigrant concentration.

Conclusion

Public policies are based on an ambivalent interpretation of how ethnic groupings are constituted (BLANC, 1990). The residential movements of immigrants, whose presence qualifies by analogy their area of residence, are viewed in different ways by policy-makers. Ethnic grouping strategies create a *protective enclave* image, which is negatively associated with the idea of a closed-in community. The emergence of immigrant neighbourhoods shows the resilience of the segregational system and demonstrates how little freedom immigrants have in their residential choices. The enclave is a *locked-in area*, and its inhabitants are, so to speak, under house arrest (BOUMAZA, 1996). In contrast to these forced or willing forms of ethnic regrouping, other strategies involve dispersion outside the area where most of the group lives. Very often, this trend is interpreted as a wish to become integrated into mainstream society. In this case, immigrants move to a neutral environment, devoid of community structures, and become *collectively invisible*, or unmarked as a community.[10] But mobility can also be used as an instrument of domination. Immigrant households are often evicted or rehoused because their dwelling is scheduled for demolition, and they are often destabilised as a result of these forced moves. Moving to neutral areas is not always synonymous with emancipation; in some cases, it can go along with a loss of familiar reference points and cause people to withdraw into their close family environment instead of joining mainstream society.

Despite these contradictory interpretations, public policy-makers opted for desegregation. As a result, new obstacles were set in the path of immigrants wishing to move. The implementation of "social and ethnic readjustment" policies in problem neighbourhoods led to increased filtering, thus limiting immigrants' housing opportunities even more. The procedures for the allocation of social housing involve the selection of candidates according to ethnic and racial criteria. Thus, under the pretext of avoiding concentration, households are banished to areas with a "bad reputation", or refused access to social housing. This style of management, which could be called "management through banishment", is reminiscent of the methods of the private sector, where the worst slums are left to those who cannot be housed in conventional dwellings, either because they cannot afford it, or because of ethnic or racial discrimination.[11]

At the same time, demand for social housing is on the rise. Between 1988 and 1992, a 37 % increase brought the number of applicants to 915,000. Immigrant households are priority recipients of social housing. More than 70 % of immigrants from North Africa,

---

[10] The fact that immigrants are not "visible" as a group does not necessarily mean that individuals themselves are not identified as immigrants.

[11] For an example of the segregational impact of different social housing allocation systems, see the study of the city of Genevilliers, in the Paris suburbs, by LÉVY (1984).

Turkey or sub-Saharan Africa apply for public housing, as opposed to 14 % of the total number of households. This trend clearly appears after examination of the files of priority applicants.[12] In 1992, 34 % of the applicants were foreign citizens, while foreigners represent 16 % of Paris's total population. They also represent 70 % of the households of five or more members, and their housing needs are specific and not always easy to meet. A consequence of the improvement of immigrants' living conditions is that their proportional presence increases in the areas where they are already numerous.

The results of anti-segregation planning policies thus seem to contradict the intention of "breaking the Ghetto"; public policy-makers are thus faced with an impossible dilemma:

—France is a multicultural society which does not recognise itself as such; ethnic origin plays a more or less explicit role in the stratification of social groups, and in that sense it partially determines a household's residential possibilities within an urban system strongly marked by segregational practices.

—Ethnic minorities are not institutionally recognised in France. For this reason, public anti-segregation policies are hampered by having to deal with populations that do not officially exist. Worse than that, these policies have led to deliberately discriminatory practices, since certain ethnic groups are barred from some public housing programmes so as to avoid the development or increase of ethnic concentrations.

—The implementation of secret immigrant quotas for access to certain social housing programmes contradicts the professed wish to reduce inequalities. The residential movements of immigrants are "ethnically" oriented so as to avoid neighbourhood conflicts between "natives" and "unwanted immigrants", and as a result, the latter end up being exiled to the areas with the worst reputation. There is a growing gap between the ethnic groups which are gradually becoming integrated into French mainstream society, and those which are rejected and form clearly identified groups, separated from the rest of society.

—Sometimes, but not always, ethnic concentration fosters the development of community structures and activities, such as shops, places of worship, neighbourhood associations, etc. However, ethnic "enclaves" in the economic sector are few and

---

[12] Source: Files of applicants for social housing in Paris, situation as of 1 September 1992, statistical appendixes submitted to the *Conseil de Paris*.

not very powerful; they concern, for instance, the Portuguese (construction industry), Asians (trade and small electronics companies) and North Africans for import and export businesses (TARRIUS, 1992). Furthermore, the tendency of ethnic communities to live and work together is countered by the determination of public authorities to enforce the principles of common law and to avoid funding associations whose activities are too strictly limited to the needs of a specific ethnic group. However, in France, for the time being, the ethnic territorialisation process has not yet reached the scope and degree of cohesiveness characteristic of the American "ghettos" and "barrios".

References

BACHMANN, C.; LEGUENNEC, N. (1996): *Violences urbaines. Ascension et chute des classes moyennes à travers 50 ans de politique de la ville*. Albin Michel, Paris.

BATTEGAY, A. (1992): "L'actualité de l'immigration dans les villes françaises: la question des territoires ethniques", *Revue Européenne des Migrations Internationales* 8, no. 2, pp. 83-98.

BERNARDOT, M. (1995): "Le mode de vie des résidents en foyers pour isolés à la Sonacotra", *Horizon*, Hors série Sonacotra, no. 2.

BESSY, P.; TABARD, N. (1996): "La concentration des qualifications sur le territoire", *Données sociales 1996*, Paris: INSEE, pp. 394-402.

BJÖRKLUND, U. (1987): "Ethnicité et État-Providence", *Revue Internationale des Sciences Sociales*, no. 111, pp. 21-33.

BLANC, M. (1990): "Du logement insalubre à l'habitat social dévalorisé. Les minorités ethniques en Allemagne, France et Grande-Bretagne", *Les Annales de la Recherche Urbaine*, no. 49, pp. 37-48.

BOUMAZA, N. (1996): "Territorialisation des Maghrébins: regroupement contraint et désir de dispersion" in Haumont, N. *La ville: agrégation et ségrégation sociales*, pp. 31-53. L'Harmattan, Paris.

BRETON, R. (1964): "Institutional completeness of ethnic communities and the personal relations of immigrants", *American Journal of Sociology* 70, pp. 193-205.

BRUN, J. (1994): "Essai critique sur la notion de ségrégation et sur son usage en géographie urbaine" in Brun, J. et C.Rhein (eds) *La ségrégation dans la ville*, pp. 21-58. L'Harmattan, Paris.

BURGESS, E.W. (1925): "The growth of the city: an introduction to a research project", in R.E. Park, E.W. Burgess and R.D. McKenzie *The City*, pp. 47-62. University of Chicago Press, Chicago (4th edition, 1967).

CASTEL, R. (1995): *Les Métamorphoses de la question sociale. Une chronique du salariat*. Fayard, Paris.

CHAMPION, J.B.; MARPSAT, M. (1996): "La diversité des quartiers prioritaires: un défi pour la politique de la ville", Economie et Statistique, no. 294-295, pp. 47-65.
CHAMPION, J.B.; GOLDBERGER, M.-F.; MARPSAT, M. (1993): "Les quartiers 'en convention'", Regards sur l'actualité, La Documentation française, no. 196.
CHEBBAH, L.L. (1996): "La politique française d'intégration, entre spécifique ou droit commun", Hommes et Migrations, no. 1203, pp. 13-18.
CHENU, A.; TABARD, N. (1993): "Les transformations socioprofessionnelles du territoire français, 1982-1990", Population 6, pp.1735-1770.
CHEVALIER, L. (1950): La formation de la population parisienne au XIXe siècle, Travaux et documents de l'INED, no. 10, PUF, Paris.
CHEVALIER, L. (1958): Classes laborieuses, classes dangereuses à Paris pendant la première moitié du XIXe siècle, Plon, Paris.
COMMISSION DE LA NATIONALITÉ (1988) Etre Français aujourd'hui et demain, Rapport de la commission de la nationalité, Paris, UGE, 10/18.
DAMAMME, D.; JOBERT, B. (1995): "La politique de la ville ou l'injonction contradictoire en politique", Revue française de science politique 45, no. 1, pp.3-30.
DE RUDDER, V. (1982): "Vivent les Ghettos?", GRECO 13, no. 4-5, pp.52-67.
DE RUDDER, V. (1993): "Le logement des immigrés"", in J. Barou and H.K. Le L'immigration entre loi et vie quotidienne. L'Harmattan, Paris.
DESPLANQUES, G.; TABARD, N. (1991): "La localisation de la population étrangère", Economie et Statistique, no. 242, p.51-62.
DESROSIÈRES, A. (1993): La politique des grands nombres. Histoire de la raison statistique. La Découverte, Paris.
DONZELOT, J.; ESTÈBE, P. (1994): L'Etat-animateur, essai sur la politique de la ville. Esprit, Paris.
DUBEDOUT, H. (1983): Ensemble, refaire la ville. Paris: La Documentation française.
DUBET, F.; LAPEYRONNIE, D. (1992): Les quartiers d'exil. Seuil, Paris.
DUNCAN, O.; DUNCAN, B. (1965): The Negro Population of Chicago: a study of residential succession. University of Chicago Press, Chicago.
GANS, H.J. (1962): The Urban Villagers. Group and Class in the Life of Italian-Americans. Free Press Glencoe, New York.
GEINDRE, F. (1993): Villes, démocratie, solidarité: le pari d'une politique, rapport au Commissariat Général au Plan, Paris: La Documentation française/Le Moniteur.
GUILLON, M. (1996): "Etrangers et Français par acquisition en France, une lente diversification sociale", Revue Européenne des Migrations Internationales 12, no. 2, pp.123-148.
GUILLON, M. (1993): "Immigration: le renfort de la polarisation parisienne, 1975-1990", Espace-Populations-Sociétés, no. 2, p.371-378.
HAUT CONSEIL À L'INTÉGRATION (1993): L'intégration à la française, Paris: UGE 10/18.
HOVANESSIAN, M. (1992): Le lien communautaire. Trois générations d'Arméniens. Armand Colin, Paris.

INSEE (1997): "Les immigrés en France", coll. *Contours et caractères*. INSEE, Paris.
JARGOWSKY, P.A (1997): *Poverty and place. Ghettos, Barrios, and the American cities*. Russell Sage Foundation, New York.
KNOX, P. (1995): *Urban Social Geography: an Introduction*. Longman Scientific & Technical (3rd edn), Harlow.
LEQUIN, Y. (1988): "Travail immigré, Français de papiers", in Y. Lequin (ed.) *La mosaïque France*. Larousse, Paris.
LÉVY, J.P. (1984): "Ségrégation et filières d'attribution des logements sociaux locatifs, l'exemple de Gennevilliers", *Espaces et Sociétés*, no. 45.
LIEBERSON, S.; WATERS, M.C. (1988): *From many strands. Ethnic and racial groups in contemporary America*. Russell Sage Foundation, New York.
LORCERIE, F. (1995): "Scolarisation des enfants d'immigrés: état des lieux et état des questions en France", *Confluences Méditerranée*, no. 14, pp.25-60.
MA MUNG, E. (1994): "L'entreprenariat ethnique en France", *Sociologie du Travail* 36, no. 2, pp.185-229.
MANSUY, M.; MARPSAT, M. (1991): "Les quartiers des grandes villes: contrastes sociaux en milieu urbain", *Economie et Statistique*, no. 245, pp.33-47.
MAUCO, G. (1932): *Les étrangers en France et leur rôle dans l'activité économique*. Armand Colin, Paris.
MILZA, P. (ed.) (1986): *Les Italiens en France de 1914 à 1940*. Ecole Française de Rome, Rome.
NOIRIEL, G. (1989): "Les espaces de l'immigration ouvrière, 1880-1930", in S. Magri and C.Topalov (eds) *Villes ouvrières, 1900-1950*. L'Harmattan, Paris.
PAUGAM, S. (1991): *La disqualification sociale. Essai sur la nouvelle pauvreté*. PUF, Paris.
PAUGAM, S. (1995): "L'habitat socialement disqualifié" in F. Ascher (ed.), *Le logement en question*, pp.213-234. Editions de l'Aube, Paris.
PETERSEN, W. (1987): "Politics and the Measurement of Ethnicity", in W. Alonso and P. Starr (eds) *The Politics of Numbers*. Russell Sage Foundation, New York.
POIRET, C. (1996): *Familles africaines en France: ethnicisation, ségrégation et communalisation*. L'Harmattan, Paris.
PONTY, J. (1988): *Polonais méconnus. Histoire des travailleurs immigrés en France dans l'entre-deux-guerres*, Paris: Publications de la Sorbonne.
PORTES, A.; JENSEN, L. (1987): "What's an ethnic enclave? The case for conceptual clarity" (commentaries on the article by Sanders and Nee), *American Sociological Review* 52, pp.768-771.
PORTES, A.; JENSEN, L. (1989): "The enclave and the entrants: patterns of ethnic enterprise in Miami before and after Mariel", *American Sociological Review* 54, pp. 929-949.
PORTES, A.; JENSEN, L. (1992): "Disproving the enclave hypothesis", (further reply to Sanders and Nee) *American Sociological Review* 57, pp. 418-420.
RAULIN, A. (1988): "Espaces marchands et concentrations urbaines minoritaires. La petite Asie de Paris", *Cahiers Internationaux de Sociologie* 85, pp. 225-242.

REMY, J. (1990): "La ville cosmopolite et la coexistence inter-ethnique", in A. Bastenier and F. Dassetto (eds) *Immigrations et nouveaux pluralismes*. De Boeck: Bruxelles.
RHEIN, C. (1994): "La ségrégation et ses mesures" in J. Brun and C. Rhein (eds) *La ségrégation dans la ville*, pp. 121-161. L'Harmattan, Paris.
SANDERS, J.M.; NEE, V. (1987): "Limits of ethnic solidarity", *American Sociological Review* 52, pp.745-773.
SANDERS, J.M.; NEE, V. (1992): "Problems in resolving the enclave economy debate", (reply to Portes and Jensen) *American Sociological Review* 57, pp. 415-417.
SIMON, P. (1992): "Belleville, quartier d'intégration", *Migrations et société* 4, no. 19, pp.45-68.
SIMON, P. (1995): "La société partagée. Relations interethniques et interclasses dans un quartier en rénovation, Belleville, Paris xxe", *Cahiers Internationaux de Sociologie* 98, p.161-190.
SIMON, P. (1996a): "Espace de vie des immigrés en France: une typologie", *Espace, Populations, Sociétés* 2-3, pp.305-314.
SIMON, P. (1996b): "Les immigrés et le logement: une singularité qui s'atténue", *Données Sociales*, INSEE, pp. 421-428.
SIMON, P.; TRIBALAT, M. (1993): "Chronique de l'immigration", *Population* 1, pp.125-182.
STATISTICS CANADA AND US BUREAU OF THE CENSUS (1993): *Challenges of Measuring an Ethnic World: Science, Politics and Reality*. US Government Printing Office, Washington.
TABARD, N. (1993): "Des quartiers pauvres aux banlieues aisées: une représentation sociale du territoire", *Economie et statistique* 10, no. 270, pp.5-22.
TANTER, A.; TOUBON, J.-C. (1995): "Vingt ans de politique française de logement social", *Regards sur l'actualité*, no. , pp.30-50
TARRIUS A. (1992): *Les fourmis d'Europe. Migrants riches, migrants pauvres et nouvelles villes internationales*. L'Harmattan, Paris.
TOPALOV, C. (1991): "Intervention au Séminaire chercheurs décideurs", *Loi d'orientation pour la ville*, METL et PCA, Recherches, no. 20, pp. 60-64.
TOUBON, J.C.; MESSAMAH, K. (1991): *Centralité immigrée. Le quartier de la Goutte d'Or*. L'Harmattan/CIEMI, Paris.
TRIBALAT, M. (1989): "Immigrés, étrangers, français: l'imbroglio statistique", *Population et Sociétés*, no. 241, pp.1-4.
TRIBALAT, M. (1991): "Combien sont les Français d'origine étrangère?", *Economie et Statistique*, no. 242, p.17-29.
TRIBALAT, M. (1993): "Les immigrés au recensement de 1990 et les populations liées à leur installation en France", *Population* 6, p.1911-1946.
TRIBALAT, M. (with SIMON, P.; RIANDEY, B.) (1996): *De l'immigration à l'assimilation. En quête sur les populations d'origine étrangère en France*. La Découverte/INED, Paris.
VIEILLARD-BARON, H. (1990): "Le ghetto: un lieu commun impropre et banal", *Les Annales de la Recherche Urbaine*, no. 49, pp.13-22.

VIEILLARD-BARON, H. (1994): *Les banlieues françaises ou le ghetto impossible*. Editions de l'Aube, Paris.
VIET (1998) *La France immigrée. Construction d'une politique 1914-1997*. Fayard, Paris.
VILLANOVA, R. DE; BEKKAR, R. (1994): *Immigration et espaces habités*. L'Harmattan/CIEMI, Paris.
VOLOVITCH-TAVARES, M.C. (1995): *Portugais à Champigny, le temps des baraques*. Autrement, Paris.
WACQUANT, L.J.D. (1992): "Pour en finir avec le mythe des 'cités-Ghettos'. Les différences entre la France et les Etats-Unis", *Les Annales de la Recherche Urbaine*, no. 54, pp. 21-29.
WALDINGER, R. (1996): "Ethnicity and Opportunity in the Plural City", in R. Waldinger and M. Bozorgmehr (eds) *Ethnic Los-Angeles*, pp. 445-479. Russell Sage Foundation, New York.
WEIL (1991): *La France et ses étrangers*, Paris : Calmann-Lévy et FNSP.
WELLMAN, B.; LEIGHTON, B. (1981): "Réseau, quartier et communauté. Préliminaire à l'étude de la question communautaire", *Espaces et Sociétés*, no. 38-39, pp.111-133.
WIEVIORKA, M. (1996): *Une société fragmentée? Le multiculturalisme en débat*. La Découverte, Paris.
WILSON, K.; PORTES, A. (1980): "Immigrant Enclaves: Labor Experiences of Cubans in Miami", *American Journal of Sociology* 86, no. 2, pp.295-319.
WUHL, S. (1996): *Insertion: les politiques en crise*. PUF, Paris.

Table 1. Housing tenure and occupancy for selected groups of immigrants, France, 1992 (%)

	Algeria	Morocco	Portugal	South-East Asia	Spain	Turkey	Sub-sahelian Africa	France
Owners	17	13	39	35	56	16	10	56
Public housing (good shape)	29	32	20	24	14	33	23	14
Private rented (good shape)	19	19	21	22	18	21	24	19
Public housing (poor quality)	17	16	4	12	4	18	12	3
Private rented (poor quality)	9	10	8	6	3	12	16	2
Migrant hostels	6	5	0	1	0	0	13	0
Grace and lodged by employers	3	5	7	2	6	1	3	6
Total	100	100	100	100	100	100	100	100
Total poor quality	29	29	16	19	10	32	31	7
Poor quality in Public Housing	55	54	29	62	40	55	37	36

Source: MGIS survey, INED with the support of INSEE, 1992.

Table 2. Immigrants by country of birth and type of neighbourhood, France, 1992 (%)

	Algeria	Morocco	Portugal	South-East Asia	Spain	Turkey	Sub-sahelian Africa	Average France
Detached home	21	22	42	21	50	19	15	32
Old	12	10	27	9	32	12	10	21
New	4	3	6	9	9	1	3	5
Public housing	47	48	25	40	18	50	34	35
Small buildings/ low concentration	8	7	6	5	4	6	6	7
Small buildings/ high concentration	14	15	6	12	2	20	5	6
Large blocks/ low concentration	4	4	3	4	1	3	3	5
Large blocks/medium concentration	8	7	4	7	2	5	5	5
Large blocks/ high concentration	4	4	1	3	1	6	4	2
Old city centre	19	16	21	11	18	17	32	16
Historical centre	11	11	14	7	13	9	18	11
Inner-city slums	6	3	2	2	1	4	7	2
Renewed city centre	8	10	8	14	9	11	9	14
Cheap rented houses	5	6	3	7	3	7	4	3
Gentrified areas	3	4	5	7	6	4	5	7
New suburbs	4	5	2	15	5	3	10	7
Total	100	100	100	100	100	100	100	100

Source : MGIS survey, INED with the support of INSEE, 1992; 1990 census, INSEE.

Table 3. Unemployment and social dissimilarity by type of neighbourhood, France, 1992 (%)

	% of immigrants	Unemployment rate (immigrants)	Over-unemployment index (immigrants) (a)	Social dissimilarity index (b)
Detached home	14.5	16	1.7	25.4
Old	11	14	1.5	22.2
New	15.2	15	1.9	26.3
Public housing	30.3	27	1.5	29.6
Small buildings/ low concentration	20	25	1.4	22.9
Small buildings/ high concentration	52	31	1.4	26.8
Large blocks/ low concentration	17.3	24	1.4	19
Large blocks/ medium concentration	35.3	27	1.5	25.7
Large blocks/ high concentration	53	30	1.4	27.3
Old city centre	28	20	2.1	36.6
Historical centre	22	18	1.8	32
Inner-city slums	61	27	1.8	49.8
Renewed city centre	22	21	1.9	30
Cheap rented houses	45	26	1.9	32.2
Gentrified areas	16	16	1.8	24.8
New suburbs	18	18	2.5	27.2

Source: MGIS survey, INED with the support of INSEE, 1992; 1990 census, INSEE.
(a) Over-unemployment index: immigrants' unemployment rate/natives' unemployment rate.
(b) Dissimilarity index between immigrants' and natives' occupational stratification (11 positions).

The study of community development in the city
Diversity as a tool

Ruth Soenen and Marc Verlot

Diversity and complexity in education

This article, focusing upon community development in urban environments, derives from research undertaken in multi-ethnic schools in Flanders. The research focused on the way pupils and teachers dealt with diversity as an overall phenomenon in social interaction. It was set up to give a new impetus to the previously rather unsuccessful implementation of intercultural education in Flanders. Intercultural education in Europe developed in the early 1970s as a pedagogical response to the influx of immigrant children in schools. Although widely promoted by teachers' unions, national governments and international bodies, intercultural education did not alter the social and cultural relations between "newcomers" and "settled pupils". The reason for this apparent failure is to be found in the fact that homogeneity is at the core of school policy and governmental policy (VERLOT/SIERENS, 1997; VERLOT/ PINXTEN, 2000). Confronted with the necessity of dealing with the needs of immigrant pupils, schools in the 1970s and 1980s started to develop a specific approach to immigrant pupils. Often this approach came down to setting immigrant pupils apart and applying a more intensive and specific programme to acquaint them with the "school culture". Adaptation to this culture in order to create a homogenous group within the school was seen as a crucial condition in order to become socially successful.

The cultural background of the immigrants was perceived as being detrimental to their chances of success in the education system. Little attention was thus paid to the social and cultural features of immigrant pupils. As a result of wider social and economic diversification, schools gradually began to take these social and cultural features into account.

As a consequence, the cultural background of immigrant pupils was seen less in terms of contributing to their educational shortcomings, but more in terms of valuable differences. It was premised that the school results of immigrant pupils would improve if the teachers integrated elements of the identity of the immigrant pupils in the learning process. Bridging the gap between the school (culture) and the home (culture) of the immigrant pupils became the central aim.[1]

Building on this set of ideas, intercultural education has developed along three lines. Originally intercultural education was (and often still is) understood as providing pupils with facts about, and the historic background of, each others' (ethnic) cultures. Culture in this perspective is perceived as a static collection of specific features linked with discrete ethnic groups (BOOS-NUNNING et al., 1986). In reaction, a number of pedagogues and teachers, believing this approach to be too cognitive and one-sided, pleaded for an approach in which pupils' attitudes would be more central. Coming from this angle, intercultural education was developed in the early 1980s to stress instead the importance of teaching tolerance and respect as a basic attitude in a multicultural society. However, for some more radical commentators (cf. STONE, 1981), teaching tolerance was insufficient to challenge the existing discrimination. Rather, they emphasised the processes of structural discrimination in society and the role of the school in this. Proponents of this perspective claimed that teachers should make existing power relations between majorities and minorities visible and counter them more explicitly by anti-racist education.

Although the three approaches to intercultural education were seen as mutually exclusive by each of their protagonists, they in fact have much more in common than is apparent at first view. Crucially, in all the approaches, adults categorised pupils as belonging to a homogeneous cultural or ethnic group with clearly distinguishable characteristics.

---

[1] SOENEN (1999b, p. 13) explains that «in many circles the starting point with regard to migrant children still goes back to the idea that these children are only determined by the breach between their home culture and school culture. They are supposed to passively undergo the messages of their home culture (their parents) and the school culture (their teachers). They are supposed to have lost their bearings and as a result they live 'in or between' two worlds». SOENEN (2000a, p. 7-8) refers among others to WEISNER et al. (1988): «An interesting piece of research into experience concerning ethnicity in schools is done by Weisner et al. Too often children are presumed to be determined by common experiences deriving from their ethnic and cultural background. In this view culture has a uniform effect on children. For Weisner, focusing on cultural identity could bring about inaccurate interpretations. Classroom modifications must be made in response to students' interest and performance rather than to isomorphism with natal cultural practice.»

Intercultural education was thought of as a way to enhance the relations between these *groups* of pupils. Little attention was given to the variety between pupils of the same ethnic group or the ways pupils develop strategies to deal with diversity. This homogenistic categorial tendency of these approaches has been increasingly questioned from the 1990s onwards, because of its inherent incapacity to take into account the ways pupils deal with the actual conditions of diversity.

Previous considerations of cultural diversity have a strong normative and prescriptive tendency. In the research undertaken, our emphasis was less upon an external *a priori* conceptualisation of intercultural education imposed on schools and their pupils. Instead it emphasised that «we need to examine how dealing with differences is given form here and now» (SOENEN 2000a, p. 1). The research looked at pupils and teachers in their daily experience of diversity. In order not to categorise ethnic groups *a priori* (as was the tendency in the aforementioned approaches to intercultural education), our focus was upon social interaction among pupils and (to a lesser extent) with the teacher (SOENEN 1998a, 2000a). Through our research, it became apparent that pupils were quite competent in dealing with diversity and developed strategies in which to manage it. These strategies are dependent on context; the application of different strategies changed according to time and place. In addition it was observed that pupils were able to shift from one mode of interaction to another or to combine different modes of interaction (DE MUNTER/SOENEN 1997; SOENEN 1998b, 1999a, b, 2000a). Influenced by the school of thought known as pragmatism, and building upon the results of the research, we claim that intercultural education should thus also start from the existing intercultural competence of pupils and teachers (VERLOT *et al.*, 2000).

From the school to the city

The social relevance behind our current research lies in rendering a new dynamic to life in the city. In particular, it is intended to generate a manual for community building. Before we explore this in the third section we will first look into some descriptions of changes in city life and consequent policy during the last decades.

Changes in the schools

Researching social interaction in Flemish schools in popular city neighbourhoods, we were confronted with the teachers' personal narratives of social geography, or more precisely of the way their schools have evolved over the last three decades. In these narratives teachers indicate two developments. They refer to the loss of Flemish pupils and the influx of immigrant pupils in their schools. This first development can for some schools be traced back to the beginning of the 1970s. In their accounts teachers explain the gradual decline of Flemish pupils through the moving of lower middle class Flemish families from popular neighbourhoods towards greener areas around the city. At the same time, the first immigrant pupils from the south of Italy, Spain, Greece, Morocco and Turkey appeared in these neighbourhoods. They were taken in by the schools first and foremost to compensate for the loss of Flemish pupils. As their numbers slowly grew, more Flemish pupils went to other schools until hardly any Flemish pupils were left and the school only attracted immigrant pupils. In schools that were confronted with the same development at a later stage, teachers no longer refer to movement as an explanation for this change. In their perception, Flemish families chose schools with fewer or no immigrant pupils, without moving from the neighbourhood. They explain this shift through Flemish parents' fears of a decline in quality of teaching. Teachers confirmed this idea of decline by referring to the difficulty of teaching pupils with another mother tongue than Dutch and/or another cultural background. Listening to the teachers' accounts, it becomes obvious that teachers themselves have at least partially generated and sustained the association between immigrant pupils and a decline in quality of teaching (VERLOT 1999a).

The second development, suggested in the teachers' accounts, became apparent in the early 1990s. Some (mostly large) schools in the aforementioned popular neighbourhoods in Antwerp and Ghent with a majority of immigrant pupils received enquiries from young Flemish families who had recently moved into the neighbourhood. These parents were almost always highly educated and had a positive opinion on issues such as multiculturalism. Gradually, this resulted in the enrolment of small numbers of Flemish pupils in these schools. At the same time principals started to reconsider the negative image their schools had in the eyes of the mainstream Flemish inhabitants. This process of reconsideration prompted the principals to develop a more positive self-perception of their own schools. They also started to look more closely at the neighbourhood where their schools were situated. Much to their surprise, they almost all came to the conclusion that contrary to their opinion, the popular neighbourhoods did not only consist of immigrant families but still contained Flemish households sending their children to schools outside the neighbourhood. As a consequence they have recently begun to develop a more open and assertive policy towards *all* the inhabitants of the neighbourhood, stressing the benefits of a heterogeneous school population.

Changes in the city

The narratives of teachers and principals can be understood as the way in which people give meaning to what is happening in their environment and the way they try to adapt and influence these general processes.

The developments indicated by the narratives of teachers and principals are sustained by quantitative socio-economic and geographical research on the city. KESTELOOT (n.d.) in his research on Brussels indicates two processes that are also valid for Antwerp and Ghent. The first process is that of suburbanisation, the second is that of the rise of the so-called "new urbanism" (*nouvelle urbanité*). The process of suburbanisation refers to two separate phenomena. The first phenomenon is that of average Belgian households[2] moving out of the city since the 1960s. The increase of average income facilitated the movement of Belgian households away from the inner city towards its greener surroundings or further outside to the countryside. Only those households who could not afford to move away stayed in the popular neighbourhoods. The second phenomenon with regard to suburbanisation was the appearance of new inhabitants. Antwerp, Brussels and Ghent attracted guest workers coming from the South of Italy, Spain, Greece, and from Morocco and Turkey. They took over the houses deserted by their former Belgian inhabitants in the cheaper, more popular neighbourhoods. At first, in the 1970s, the immigrants rented houses. However, from the beginning of the 1980s they started to buy the houses as they realised that going back to their homelands was increasingly a more long-term project and vision. Furthermore, their children were settling into the "new" environment. The influx of immigrants and their settlement resulted in a cultural diversification of the popular neighbourhoods. Unlike other cities in Europe these occurrences never led to ghettoisation-like processes as some less well-off and/or older Belgian families stayed in these neighbourhoods.

With the movement of the average Belgian household out of the city, politicians became less interested in the city. City policy was increasingly dependent on the vagaries of market influences. This often led to huge speculation, as for example in central Brussels where rows

---

[2] The term "Belgian households" describes processes that apply for Antwerp, Ghent and Brussels, while "Flemish households" refers only to the cities of Antwerp and Ghent.

of (sometimes historically and aesthetically very valuable) houses were left uninhabited, to decline until they were suitable only for demolition. They were gradually replaced by offices, shops, hotels or banks. Reading this trend from a more cultural point of view, the inner city was reshaped into an area limited to work and consumption. This led to a temporal fragmentation of the inner city into a business and shopping district as opposed to a residential area. Whilst it was crowded and busy during the day, it was deserted in the evening and at the weekends. Gradually the inner city became an area that was associated with alienation and anomie.

Due to the economic growth in Europe at the end of the 1980s, a new development was set in motion, which resulted in a return of higher income households to the city. KESTELOOT (n.d.) links this return («new urbanism») with more general phenomena including increasing flexibility of production and consumption on the one hand and geographical competition on the other hand. The expansion of the economy introduced new capital, new (often smaller) offices and new inhabitants in the former popular neighbourhoods. This undeniably revived the popular neighbourhoods, but at the same time started to push away the lower income inhabitants. The result was that the social division of the city between lower and higher incomes was strengthened. At first sight, this influx of new young households in the popular neighbourhoods seems to have strengthened but also changed the nature of the social division. In the 1980s, the central problem was the tension between low-income Belgian households and immigrant households. However, the influx of higher income households since the 1990s created pressure on the housing market, thereby causing an added tension of social polarisation between lower and (mainly Belgian) higher income households. The overall consequence of these changes in the city is that social and cultural diversity has grown considerably over the last forty years. At the same time social relations have become increasingly more complex, crosscutting the divisions firstly between immigrant and Belgian families and secondly between lower income immigrant and Belgian families and higher income Belgian families in the same neighbourhoods.

Changes in policy

When policy makers started to elaborate city renewal programmes around the end of the 1980s, they were confronted with two sets of problems: social problems referring to the social dualisation of the city, and more general infrastructural problems. As such, city renewal policy developed along these two lines. Socially, the problem was formulated in terms of the polarisation between the low-income Belgian and immigrant families living in the same neighbourhoods. The first social welfare programmes were developed to support each of these groups apart, aiming at reducing the tension between them. This led to a categorial approach in the social programmes. Infrastructurally, there was the need to guarantee a certain degree of mobility in the cities that had been suffocated by the increase of traffic. Furthermore, there was a drive towards the revaluation of historical buildings and the introduction and creation of open common recreational space. Up until the mid-1990s these two programmes followed their own logic, their own planning and their own goals, and were seldom integrated.

The growing tension and antagonisms between these two policy lines soon became apparent and obliged policy makers to reconceptualise city renewal policy. Following the process of gentrification induced by the influx of new young Belgian households from the 1990s onwards, policy plans were designed such that the idea of the inner city as a living environment became central again. A living environment was understood as an environment in which work, living and leisure could be combined. The question then became one of revitalising the inner city by diversifying and combining economic and social functions. The social problem was reformulated. To revitalise the city, it was thought that there was a need to diversify the social fabric by attracting even more middle and high income households. Its most direct consequence was that the social and infrastructural programmes were intertwined in relation to the wider attitude to the city, one that saw the city as a "living environment". It is in the context of this shift of ideas that the concepts of "communities" and "community development" were reintroduced in city renewal policy.

The reintroduction of the "community" in the framework of the revitalisation idea has direct consequences for the way policy makers perceive and conceptualise communities and community development. Policy makers are confronted with the division created by the influx of higher income households and the consequent processes of social exclusion. As such they define city renewal policy in terms of economic revitalisation while at the same time combatting the growing social division.

Diversity and complexity in the city

To get a more thorough insight into the diversity and complexity of social relationships in the city, we need to take into account the social interaction of people and the meaning they give to the changes described in general trends (SOENEN, 1998b). The following section examines some examples of research that studies how people live in those contexts as described by the quantitative socio-economic and geographical research we dealt with before.

Research into meaning and social interaction

The narratives of teachers and principals about the movement of pupils in their schools are confirmed by "top-down" socio-economic and geographical research. However, to grasp the meaning of these processes of moving, diversification and dualisation for the people involved, we need to complement this research with a bottom-up approach. Some anthropologists and sociologists have looked in depth at how different groups coped in daily life with social and cultural changes in Belgian cities. Originally, emphasis was placed upon the experiences and perceptions of specific groups in the city. LEMAN, for example (1982, 1989), compared the ways that groups of Sicilians adapted to the Brussels context their behaviour and actions in their home towns in Sicily. HERMANS (1994) again focused on a specific group, in this instance second generation Moroccans, studying their particular processes of acculturating.

More recent research tends to integrate network analysis into its approaches. This involves an emphasis on relationships between individuals and interactions within or starting from the diversity of neighbourhoods, rather than the more group-specific emphasis of before. This approach is demonstrated by BLOKLAND-POTTERS (1998) in her study of the diversity and complexity of community life in the Hillesluis popular neighbourhood in Rotterdam (the Netherlands). In her study, Blokland-Potters distinguishes four types of networks evident in social interaction. Networks differ in terms of frequency of social contacts, the degree of specialisation, the density and their range.[3]

---

[3] The first type is that of the "new urbans". These are young households with a middle or higher income and a high educational level. She characterises these "new urbans" by their segregated network of social interaction: playing tennis with one person, going out with a second and studying with a third (1998, p. 78). The strong specialisation of network relations leads to segregation. The multitude of social relations leads to a low contact frequency, but is maintained over a wide reach, going beyond the limits of the neighbourhood. They find themselves in opposition to the "Janssens" in the same neighbourhood; normal people with normal lives, neither highly educated nor uneducated. They know their neighbours but do not have frequent contacts with them; their network is relatively broad, but nevertheless defined by national or cultural boundaries. The third type of network is formed by the "religiously active and the peergroups". For

These networks lead to different ideas of community or of what constitutes community. Blokland-Potters' study is particularly noteworthy because it both complements and nuances the external categorisations of people into ethnic and socio-economic groups. It tells us something about the neighbourhood as social phenomenon and about the way people create an idea of community through their personal relations with their neighbours; insights that cannot be gathered solely from statistic data, nor from a more qualitative group approach.

Echoes in the public debate

Some aspects of the complex social interaction in popular neighbourhoods are strongly echoed in the public debate on the contemporary city. As such they have an important impact on a second group of actors who give shape to life in the city: the policy makers. One of the central issues in the contemporary public debate is the multicultural character of the city. The rise of this topic seems to have been enhanced by the influx of immigrants, but also by some of the "new urbans" who position themselves as active participants in this debate. Blokland-Potters characterises the «new urbans» by their segregated network of social interaction. In general, some of these «new urbans» perceive the heterogeneous, multicultural character of the city as an attraction and have a generally positive attitude towards the presence of immigrant families. (Little is known about the way immigrant families perceive these young Belgian households.) As these households are often highly educated and politically rather "leftish", they try to counter the anti-immigrant discourse in popular neighbourhoods, although being a minority in terms of actual numbers. When walking through popular neighbourhoods in Antwerp and Ghent, for example, one can recognise their houses by the posters on windows proclaiming the benefits of multiculturalism or making a clear anti-racist statement. New urbans are often very well represented on residents' committees and all sorts of action committees to enhance life in the neighbourhood. By taking this public stance, new urbans directly confront and come into opposition with the anti-multicultural discourse of the lower income Belgian households that have been sharing these neighbourhoods

---

these people, contacts are more frequent, dense and less specialised. The fourth type is that of the isolated "new poor" who form small networks that are not specialised and have a low density.

with immigrant families for the last three decades. The antimulticultural discourse becomes apparent in interviews. When for example interviewers introduce themselves as doing research on social life in the neighbourhood or when mentioning the term "social", they are often immediately negatively associated with a pro-immigrant stance or as someone who wants to create or sustain a pro-multicultural picture of the neighbourhood.

The public debate on multiculturalism on the other hand is not solely the result of neighbourhood discourses. In the public debate on the city and city policy local discourses interact with wider political and more fundamental cultural discourses and practices. In terms of political discourse we need to mention the impact of the Vlaams Blok, an extreme right wing nationalistic and xenophobic party, influential since the latter half of the 1980. It started its spectacular rise by playing on the discontent of Belgian lower income households. Over the last ten years, these households have gained gradual support in their anti-multiculturalist discourse from higher income, often more middle aged households, settled in the greener, more affluent outskirts of the cities or in the surrounding municipalities.[4] Although not sustained by factual research, one of us (Verlot) suspects that this alliance might rest on family ties that create a virtual solidarity between low-income Belgian households in the city and higher income Belgian households in the periphery or outside the city. They share the idea that communities are built upon the sharing of the same values and daily life practices. Social and cultural diversity is seen as endangering and corrupting the basics of community life and leading to alienation.

Mainstream policy makers publicly oppose the xenophobic choices of the Vlaams Blok and adopt in reaction a more pro-multiculturalist stance. However, policy practice shows in its conceptualisations of community, the belief that diversity is antagonistic to community development. The reason for this inconsistency lies in the conceptions the Flemish policy élite use in developing policy (VERLOT 1999a). Ethnographic research on the cultural intuitions of the Flemish policy élite shows that policy is built on the idea that society is composed of different ethnic-cultural groups. These groups are seen as homogeneous and characterised by specific cultural features. This predisposition strengthens the idea that communities are based on homogeneous social and cultural features.

---

[4] A clear indication of this tendency can be found in the rising number of votes in these areas for the Vlaams Blok.

Homogeneous thinking in community development policy

When it comes to formulating policy, policy makers choose the multicultural discourse in public, positioning themselves clearly against the anti-migrant discourse of the Vlaams Blok. Despite this stance, their strategies and actions in practice paradoxically show much more a disposition to take over the basic concept of homogeneity as the basis for community life and community development. As a result, policy planners as well as social workers generally define social life in categorial terms, with the city as a totality of different homogeneous communities, each with their own ethnic and cultural features. This echoes the micro-tendencies as shown in education and policy before. Social programmes in city renewal policy in Flanders have incorporated this categorial homogenistic view. They aim at strengthening the internal ties of these different ethnic communities on the one hand, and at enhancing the relations between these communities on the other hand. As such they reinforce the central antagonism between "diversity" and "community", where diversity is associated with segregation and alienation.

This idea of a conceptual antagonism between "diversity" and "community" has a long history. It can for instance also be found in urban studies such as those of the Chicago School (ca. 1910-1930). Researchers from the Chicago School took social interactions as a central point of interest and research into the city (SOENEN, 2000b, p. 3-6). Social (inter)actions were linked with a spatial context. Researchers from this school had a particular interest in the nature of social ties in what they saw as the "modern, fragmented" city. The notion of "community" was always present in their analysis and reflection. In the different researches of the Chicago School, a community was defined in terms of neighbourhood. A geographical unity thus became synonymous with a cultural unity. At the heart of this conceptualisation lay the idea that a community is to be recognised as a cultural homogeneous group with shared ideas and practices. Conceptualising community as such, Chicago School researchers were unable to transcend the idea of a central opposition between *Gemeinschaft*, which was seen as urban and modern, and *Gesellschaft*, referring to the country and the traditional lifestyle (cf. LEVINE, 1971; TÖNNIES, 1955). Park and Burgess stated that the development of the city inevitably leads to a competition for scarce goods like houses, which results in a selection of neighbourhoods with specific social characteristics: the central business district, around which lies a zone of decay, followed by the popular zones where workers live, and the residential zone. Wirth introduced the association between heterogeneity, fragmentation and segregation, again depicting them as natural processes. In his view the high number of heterogeneous persons in the city generates more superficial and rational relationships between people: "the multitude of persons in interaction necessitates a narrowing down of contacts" (HANNERZ, 1980, p. 60, cited by SOENEN, 2000b, p. 5). The physical proximity of living close together goes hand in hand with more distant social relationships. This diversification causes disintegration and leads to social fragmentation, which in the end generates segregation.

In conclusion, it is clear that the Chicago school considered the heterogeneous character only as a negative feature of modern urban life. In their view only homogeneous categorisation led to community construction, whereas heterogeneity led to fragmentation and alienation. ABU-LUGHOD (1991, p. 270, cited by BLOKLAND-POTTERS 1998, p. 30) makes this very clear: "Indeed, underlying the preoccupation of early Chicago School founders with the differences between urban and rural ways of life was a concern that city life would destroy the foundations of the community". Drawing on social Darwinism, they presented these processes as a natural evolution. Although they made a clear attempt to conceptualise urban communities in their own context, they did not oppose the essentially negative perceptions of modernity and the city as we find them in the founding fathers of European sociology such as TÖNNIES (1887(1955)), whose ideas about community were strongly influenced by the underlying fear of modernity of which the city was seen as a symbol. MAZLISH (1989, cited by BLOKLAND-POTTERS 1998, p. 29, footnote 2) sees the early sociologists' tendency to oppose modernity and community as the result of the cultural influence of eighteenth and nineteenth century literary tradition which idealised rural life. REYNOLDS (1997) traces the conceptualisation of *Gesellschaft* versus *Gemeinschaft* even further back and situates it in the historiography of the Late Middle Ages between a *Territorialverband* (group of shared territory) that spatialises its virtual existence and a non-territorial *Personenverband* (grouping by personal ties) that substantialises its identity around non-territorial symbols. The conclusion is that the conception of a traditional homogeneous community as opposed to the heterogeneous modern one was clearly influenced by cultural fears of modernity which were projected by researchers on their conception of city life.[5] As such they bear in them a strong cultural bias, marginalising community development in city life.

---

[5] This line of thought was pushed to its extreme by the anthropologist Robert Redfield in his folk–urban continuum. On the one side he situated the primitive society and

Diversity as a tool for community building

Analogous with our research on intercultural education in schools, our research on community development in the city does not start from an *a priori* conceptualisation of community development. We look at the daily experience of diversity in the city. Using this more micro-oriented approach to social relationship building, the importance of divisions of other than socio-economic variation becomes clear. Our main criticism of contemporary city renewal programmes is directed to the fact that the heterogeneity and complexity of daily life are not taken into account. As a consequence, existing dynamics that manifest themselves in daily life are overlooked and competencies are ignored.

Using an ethnographic approach (SOENEN, 2000b) we describe the daily interaction to find out what binds people in diversified neighbourhoods. The research focuses on the way people deal with differences and on what these differences mean to them (SOENEN, 1998a). In order to allow heterogeneity and complexity into the analysis, the research places the emphasis on "interaction", both conceptually to the "what" of the study (in this case community development) as well as methodologically in relation to the "how", i.e. how the research is carried out. The interaction of the researcher with the people involved is the main instrument in this approach. It does not focus on the background of the agents, nor on the history or the morphology of the neighbourhood. It looks at the different specificities of the actors only on a secondary basis, with primacy of focus on the created experiences gained from interaction between people (SOENEN, 2000a, b).

This study of social interactions of individuals combines the use of different methods that we operationalised into:

—Interviewing a diversity of persons who are contacted through a diversity of channels with the aim to recruit as broadly as possible;
—Participant observation of meeting places where diversity manifests itself in daily life;
—Following the daily activities of a limited number of individuals (SOENEN, 2000b, p. 16).

---

on the other side the modern city. Folk societies were described as small, isolated, homogeneous, solidary, non-literate and static. Processes of individualisation, secularisation and disorganisation transformed these village societies into the heterogeneous and mobile modern city (PAPOUSEK, 1982).

These three "tracks" come, in our mind, the closest to the central research question. The priority lies with a more thorough understanding of the meaning of daily phenomena, rather than on the (analytical) explanation of these phenomena. As such the research seeks to contribute to a more complex and differentiated perception of daily life, which will enable us to formulate policy recommendations with regard to community building.

Contemporary city renewal policy, although choosing to reinforce diversity, still reflects homogenistic views ignoring the complexity of social reality. Legitimisation is found in existing and widely known scientific explanations which use a *priori* conceptualisations of community life, strongly influenced by cultural and historical presuppositions about modernity and the city. Through our kind of ethnographic research that strongly focuses upon the micro-level of social interactions of individuals, we want to do justice to the heterogeneity and complexity of community life in the city. As demonstrated in application to both the micro-level of education systems and the more macro-level of 'community' development, we aim to challenge the existing conceptions and policies which negate diversity. A more thorough understanding of the existing heterogeneity and complexity can show the way in which diversity, as a main feature of contemporary urban life, can be used as a tool, not a hurdle to be overcome, for successful community building.

References

ABU-LUGHOD, J.L. (1991): *Changing cities: Urban sociology*. Harper Collins, New York.
BOOS-NUNNING, U. et al. (1986): *Towards intercultural education: A comparative study of the education of migrant children in Belgium, England, France and the Netherlands*. Centre for Information on Language Teaching and Research, London.
BLOKLAND-POTTERS, T. (1998): *Wat stadsbewoners bindt. Sociale relaties in een achterstandswijk*. Kok Agora, Kampen.
DE MUNTER, K.; SOENEN, R. (1997): "Het dagelijks leven in de school". In: S. Sierens and M. Verlot (ed.), *Cultuurstudie 3. Themanummer: Intercultureel onderwijs*, pp. 87-111.
HANNERZ, U. (1980): "Chicago Ethnographers". In: *Exploring the City. Inquiries toward an Urban Anthropology*, ed. Ulf Hannerz. Columbia University Press, New York, pp. 19-58.
HERMANS, P. (1994): "Opgroeien als Marokkaan in Brussel, een antropologisch onderzoek over de educatie, de leefwereld en de inpassing van Marokkaanse jongens". In: *Cultuur en migratie*, Brussel.

KESTELOOT, C. (n.d.): "Le problématique de l'intégration sociale des jeunes urbains: une analyse géographique du cas bruxellois". In: *Changes in society: Crime and Criminal Justice in Europe.* Volume I: *Crime and insecurity in the city*, ed. C. Fijnaut et al. Kluwer rechtswetenschappen, Antwerp, pp. 113-129.
LEMAN, J. (1982): *Van Caltanisetta naar Brussel en Gent. Een antropologische studie in de streek van herkomst en inhet gastland bij Siciliaanse migranten.* Acco, Leuven.
LEMAN, J. (1987): *From challenging to challenged culture.* Leuven University Press, Leuven.
LEVINE, D.L. (ed.) (1971): *Georg Simmel on Individuality and Social Forms.* Chicago University Press, Chicago.
MAZLISH, B. (1989): A new science: the breakdown of connections and the birth of sociology. Oxford University Press, Oxford.
PAPOUSEK, D.A. (1982): "Robert Redfield (1897-1958)". In: *Beroep: antropoloog. Vreemde volkeren, visies en vooroordelen*, ed. G. Banck and B. van Heijningen. Uitgeverij Intermediair, Amsterdam/Brussel, pp. 93-110.
REYNOLDS, S. (1997): "The Historiography of the Medieval State". In: *Companion to Historiography*, ed. M. Bentley. Routledge, London, pp. 117-138.
SOENEN, R. (1998a): "Wetenschappelijk onderzoek vanuit een pragmatische benadering van intercultureel onderwijs". Mimeo, Steunpunt ICO, Universiteit Gent.
SOENEN, R. (1998b): "Creatieve en dynamische processen in het alledaagse leven. Een inspiratiebron voor intercultureel onderwijs". In: *Cultuur en macht. Over identiteit en conflict in een multiculturele wereld*, ed. R. Pinxten and G. Verstraete. Houtekiet, Antwerpen-Baarn, pp. 273-302.
SOENEN, R. (1999a) *Over Galliers en managers. Bouwstenen voor intercultureel leren.* Steunpunt ICO, Universiteit Gent.
SOENEN, R. (1999b): "Creativity and Competencies in Everyday School Life. Towards a Pragmatic and Dynamic Perspective on (Intercultural) Education". Paper presented at Seminar "Ethnography and Education: European Perspectives." University of Padua, Italy, 29-30 October.
SOENEN, R. (2000a): "Daily Life has Little Patience with Educational Practice". Paper presented at "Ethnography and Education Conference", University of Oxford, UK. 11-12 September.
SOENEN, R. (2000b): "Verscheidenheid als instrument voor gemeenschapsopbouw. Rapport 1. Tussentijds verslag onderzoeksproject i.o.v het Sociaal Impulsfonds". Mimeo, Steunpunt ICO, Universiteit Gent.
STONE, M. (1981): *The Education of the Black Child in Britain: The Myth of multiracial education.* s.l.: Fontana paperbacks.
TÖNNIES, F. (1955): *Community and Association.* Routledge, London.
VERLOT, M. (1996): "The school, ethnic minorities and the local community. Towards a conflict of interest?" In: *Forum of education*, 51, 2, pp. 88-94.
VERLOT, M. (1999): "Desegregatie, gemeenschapsvorming en (multi)cultuur". In: T. Bossuyt (ed.), *Vlaggen en Wimpels. Een pilootproject rond actieve kunstbeoefening*, CVA-cahiers, pp. 44-57.

VERLOT, M. (1999b): "Allochtonen in het onderwijs. Een politiek-antropologisch onderzoek naar het integratie- en onderwijsbeleid in de Franse en Vlaamse Gemeenschap van België". Gent, universiteit Gent: onuitgegeven proefschrift.
VERLOT, M.; SIERENS, S. (1997): "Intercultureel onderwijs vanuit een pragmatisch perspectief". In: S. Sierens and M. Verlot (ed.), *Cultuurstudies 3, themanummer intercultureel onderwijs*, pp. 130-178.
VERLOT, M.; PINXTEN, R. (2000): "Intercultural education and complex instruction. Some remarks and questions from an anthropological perspective on learning". In: *Intercultural Education*, 11, supplement, pp. 7-14.
VERLOT, M.; SIERENS, S.; SOENEN, R.; SUIJS, S. (2000): *Intercultureel onderwijs: leren in diversiteit*. Gent, Universiteit Gent: Steunpunt intercultureel onderwijs.
WEISNER, T.; GALLIMORE, R.; JORDAN, C. (1988): "Unpacking Cultural Effects on Classroom Learning: Native Hawaiian Peer Assistance and Child-Generated Activity". In: *Anthropology and Education Quarterly*, 19, pp. 326-353.

The Latinisation of the United States: social inequalities and cultural obsessions*

James Cohen

> you thought Mexico represented your past
> & now you're realizing Mexico is your future
> you thought there was a border between the 1st & the 3rd worlds
> & now you're realizing you're part of the 3rd world
> & your children are hanging out with us
> & your children & us are plotting against you
> hey mister, eeeh mister... mister
> & suddenly you woke up
> & it was too late to call the priest, the cops or the psychiatrist
> ay, qué pinche sustote te pegaste
> y en español
> —Guillermo Gómez-Peña
> "Border Brujo Programme Notes" (1988-89)
> *Warrior for Gringostroika*

Is the US empire, seemingly invincible from without, in the process of dissolving from within, under the weight of a Latino "minority" destined to become —at least in the southwestern US— a majority or even a new "nation"? Such a prophecy may be intriguing to some futurologists, but it is, to say the least, premature or evidence of a feverish imagination. Nonetheless, it cannot be denied that the United States is undergoing a gradual and profound transformation that could fairly be referred to as "Latinisation". While demographic indicators leave no doubt of this, it is less easy to grasp the cultural and political implications of this phenomenon. At the centre of public debate are questions such as the status of the Spanish language with respect to

---

* An earlier version of this paper was published in French in *Actuel-Marx*, number 27, March 2000 (issue entitled *L'hégémonie américaine*).

dominant English and the representation of interests attributed to Latinos as a "community". These questions often become obsessions and serve only to mask or divert attention from the great difficulties of socio-economic integration experienced by a major portion of the Latino population. These difficulties do not arise out of some mythical "clash of cultures" but out of the model of social exclusion that prevails in US society.

Latinisation as a media event

In its issue of July 12, 1999, *Newsweek* published a lead story entitled "Latin USA" with a cover photo of three young Latinos: a writer, a singer and a boxer. The subtitle invited readers to find out "How Young Hispanics are Changing America". The table of contents draws attention to the story as follows:

> Hispanics are hip, hot and about to make history. By 2005, Latino Americans will be the nation's largest minority, helping set the pace in popular culture and presidential politics. A portrait of the young Generation Ñ, its rising stars and how it'll change not just how America looks but how we see ourselves.

The lead article begins with a scene of daily life on Miami's Calle Ocho, in the heart of Little Havana. A group of Cuban demonstrators protests vociferously against the violence used by the Coast Guard the day before, while apprehending six Cuban refugees on a Florida beach. Among the bystanders spotted by the author are a group of Honduran employees of a religious bookstore, some Argentinian businessmen and several Salvadorean construction workers eating *pupusas*. A local record shop blasts *merengue* into the street while a group of elderly Cubans playing dominoes in nearby Máximo Gómez Park join in with the protestors, crying out *"Libertad! Libertad!"*

The author's strategy is clearly to evoke a place —which could just as well have been Los Angeles, San Antonio, New York or Boston— that is culturally and politically under strong Latino influence. The rapid increase in population of Hispanic origin, through immigration and through high birth rates, is compared by the author to the great wave of European immigration at the turn of the twentieth century, because it "has injected a new energy into the nation's cities". Latinos are "filling churches, building businesses and celebrating their Latin heritage". They are becoming "a potent, increasingly unpredictable political force", since younger Latinos are less attached to any given party than their parents. "Could this be the face of America's future?" asks the author rhetorically, and she replies: "Better believe it".

She then asks, "Is the rest of America ready" for so much change? The answer is both yes and no. On the one hand, there is a minority of Anglos who have taken advantage of growing Latin influence to learn about Latino culture by taking dancing lessons, Spanish classes or learning to cook Latin dishes. Not only for this particularly motivated portion of the population but for broader sectors as well, "All things Latin suddenly seem cool". The presence of Latinos in mass media culture is becoming commonplace, as the Ricky Martin phenomenon illustrates. At the same time, however, Latinos continue to be stereotyped in various (and contradictory) ways: as undocumented immigrants, as gangsters or, in a different vein, as entertainers. At the same time, the author notes, the question of immigration is less and less a matter of consensus; the idea of a Latin "invasion" has gained credibility in some circles.

In conclusion, the author asserts that Latinos constitute a new breed of immigrants to the United States: they do not need to assimilate to the mainstream culture because in many ways they already belong to it and can therefore influence it from within. As the millennium closes, she concludes, "a new nation is being born".

Although *Newsweek*'s journalistic style is apparently allergic to any kind of theorisation pertinent to critical thought, the author generates an implicit theory of the changes now occurring: US society is developing not only a new "self-image" but also a new mode of incorporation of foreign populations. The type of assimilation that was expected of earlier European immigrants is no longer on the agenda. Although Latinos to some extent do blend into the melting pot, they are not content to do so in a way that effaces their cultural heritage, and so they are changing the content of the melting pot from within. (Here again, the Ricky Martin "crossover" phenomenon is an eloquent example.)

These insights seem generally on target. However, the article clearly sins by omission by avoiding any serious mention of the problems of socio-economic integration that many if not most Latinos are experiencing today —a circumstance which cannot fail to affect the kind of incorporation of Latinos that is occurring. *Newsweek* prefers to shine light on those who have succeeded in sports, show business or corporate life, hence the eight full pages devoted to the so-called "Generation Ñ". Here the *parti pris* of *Newsweek*, typical in this respect of many mainstream periodicals, shows through clearly: better to avoid calling attention to the large numbers of poor and excluded people among Latinos than to suggest that US society is ripe not only with "cultural change" but also with growing class division.

In this relatively consensual vision of Latinisation, it is taken as inevitable that Latinos are to become more and more present in cultural and political life. The journalists' implicit, vaguely "multicultural", ideology posits an "encounter" among peoples and cultures, but it removes most of the sharp edges from the process. The essential point is that "we" US citizens (implicitly, the white, Anglophone majority), are destined to become more like "them" (the Latinos) and they more like us. However, it is worth considering the viewpoint of performance artist and poet Guillermo Gómez-Peña, who has dedicated a career to sabotaging this edulcorated version of reality: "Like the United Colors of Benetton ads," he writes, "a utopian discourse of sameness helps to erase all unpleasant stories. The message becomes a refried colonial idea: if we merely hold hands and dance the mambo together, we can effectively abolish ideology, sexual and cultural, politics, and class differences" (GÓMEZ-PEÑA, 1993, p. 57).

Fantasies of revenge and invasion

Increasing media attention to the presence of Latinos in the US reflects the widespread perception that Latinos' numbers are growing fast. As anyone can observe today, there is a rapid expansion of the population of Latin American origin in the US today. According to the 1990 census, there were more than 22 million Latino inhabitants, or about 9.9 per cent of the total population of the country (foreigners included). According to recent figures provided by the US CENSUS BUREAU (September 1999), there are 31 million Latinos living in the US, or about 11.5 per cent of the overall population. Their demographic growth is more rapid than other categories of the population, not only because of immigration, which remains abundant (in absolute terms and by comparison to any other country in the world) and largely uncontrolled, but also because of a much quicker rate of "natural" growth than among other groups. According to the projections of the Census Bureau, in the year 2050, 24.5 per cent of the inhabitants of the US will be Latinos, while "Caucasians" will have been reduced to a thin majority of 52.8 per cent (quoted in SUÁREZ-OROZCO, 1998, p. 5). In a few years, Latinos will be more numerous than African Americans and will thus have become the largest "minority" in the country. In certain states of the southwestern US, in particular California, they may become the majority within several decades, while whites have already descended below the symbolic 50 per cent level. The "demographic Latinisation", in Mike Davis' expression, is proceeding apace (DAVIS, 1999, p. 5).

But above and beyond such figures, what are the implications of the growing Latin presence? What intrigues —or terrifies— certain observers is the idea that Latinisation could provoke radical cultural and political changes in US society. One imagined scenario involves the accumulation in the southwest of a majority that is not only Spanish-speaking but also open to the geopolitical influence of Mexico and other Latin American countries. Such a possibility was invoked with pride and defiance by the separatist wing of the Chicano movement in the 1960s and 70s. Certain conservatives invoke it today, with horror of course, fearing that the southwest might turn into a third-world, irredentist "Trojan horse". In 1994, young student demonstrators in California were seen displaying the Mexican flag and this image seemed to lend credibility to such conservative nightmare scenarios. A similar fantasy has appeared among certain conservative Congressmen who evoke with fear and disgust the possible emergence of "another Quebec" in Puerto Rico, if ever that territory were to become the 51st state of the union, as at least 45 per cent of the Puerto Rican electorate wishes (see COHEN, 1999).

For the moment, the political incorporation of Puerto Rico seems quite improbable, because of the opposition of these very same conservative legislators, among other reasons. As for the project of a secession of irredentist Hispanic states in the southwest, it is pure political fiction; since the decline of the Chicano movement in the 70s, the demand for a separate state —never accepted nor even clearly understood by most Chicano militants at the time— is no longer seriously formulated by anyone. The youths who demonstrated in California with the Mexican flag were not irredentists; in spite of their provocative choice of a symbol, they were mostly interested in securing recognition of their basic citizenship rights, which Proposition 187, the anti-immigrant referendum held in California in 1995, clearly threatened by designating all Mexicans and Mexican-Americans as potential suspects and thus as scapegoats.

Those who enjoy conjuring up far-out future scenarios are further stimulated by the idea that Latinos might soon form a cohesive electoral bloc, in an area not limited to the southwest, but which could also include Hispanic populations in Chicago, New York, Washington, Boston and (in spite of particular circumstances) Miami. In this scenario, which takes into account the fact that Latinos, taken collectively, are disproportionately confronted with problems of socio-economic integration, they are seen as tending naturally to evolve into a progressive vanguard in the struggle to restore and expand the welfare state, reinforce public education and possibly bring about more radical changes. This hypothesis, however, does not appear very realistic in the foreseeable future because it fails to take into account the diversity of political currents that exist within the Latino population. There are, of course, many more Democratic than Republican voters among Latinos, and a more frequent expression of social-democratic aspirations among Latinos than among other groups. It is also true that certain lobbying groups that articulate and defend Latino collective interests formulate demands that suggest a social-democratic orientation. But there is also a strong conservative current among Latinos —and not just among Cuban exiles!— as witnessed by the fact that the Republican Party is attempting, not without success, to incorporate large numbers of Latinos into its ranks. The idea of a "progressive" or left-wing Latino political bloc will be plausible only when the idea of a nationally-based movement for social change itself becomes more than a mere chimera.

Above and beyond these extreme but largely baseless scenarios, the time is ripe to give more realistic content to what David Gutiérrez calls "the transformation of social space" in the US under the impact of Latinos (GUTIÉRREZ, 1998). In the present text I will examine some tendencies, clearly visible today, that could lead to serious conflicts in the future. At stake are the US's mode(s) of managing linguistic and ethnic diversity and its prevailing model of socio-economic integration.

The language question

What is the significance of the fact that Spanish is emerging as the second language of US society, in particular as the language of the street and of trade in several major urban zones and other areas, including a large strip of territory along the Mexican border? Can it be said that the presence of Spanish marks the emergence of a different *culture*? Much depends on how one defines the notion of linguistic difference. The borders that are perceived to exist between different languages as emblems of cultural difference can be seen largely as constructions of social actors, and in that respect are simply part and parcel of broader processes of "ethnicisation" (see BARTH, 1969). Observing the situation in countries as different as Canada, Belgium, Spain or ex-Yugoslavia, one may have the impression that conflicts of cultures and languages have an "objective" character, since they can give rise to inter-ethnic confrontation that sometimes degenerates into violence and may even taken on a genocidal nature. However, linguistic conflicts become radicalised only when the political dynamics of the countries concerned drift toward ethnic conflict; the question is at least as much one of *dynamics* as of "objective conditions". Negotiated and relatively consensual solutions can in many cases be found, as the examples of Canada and Spain illustrate. In other words, the linguistic question constitutes a contested terrain which is not "cultural" in any immediate way but above all political: it furnishes a cultural pretext for those who seek to provoke political division rather than seeking more harmonious forms of coexistence.

Since the question of the Spanish language in the US constitutes, precisely, a contested terrain, it is difficult to find reliable information about the "balance of forces" between Spanish and English. Those who wish to prove the political point that English is "losing ground", that the country is in danger of "losing its identity", and that an "invasion" is occurring and that it "needs to be stopped", always brandish figures to the effect that there are millions of inhabitants who do not speak English; that the number is growing; and that these figures indicate a increasing and conscious refusal of immigrants to adapt to the prevailing cultural norms. One Congressman clearly influenced by the "English Only" movement, Bob Goodlatte, made the dire prediction that by 2000 there would be more than 40 million Americans who do not master English (cf. CRAWFORD n.d.). Those who seek, on the contrary, to de-dramatise the question, cite figures tending to show that Latinos of the second or third generation do not always retain their Spanish and often master English at least as well as Spanish. This thesis appears more convincing, since it is well known that bilingual education programmes, where they still exist, are not conceived to perpetuate the practice of languages of origin but rather to facilitate pupils' access to the country's dominant language, English. James Crawford points out that in 1990, of the 31 million people who had been residing in the US for at least five years and who affirmed that they spoke another language than English, 25 million also said that they spoke English "well" or "very well" (CRAWFORD n.d.). It is nonetheless true that the abundant influx of new immigrants, particularly from Mexico, as well as the constitution of urban areas where Spanish rather than English is practised in the streets and in daily commercial life, often gives the impression that a profound linguistic change is in the cards. This too may be true, but one need not conclude that the US is "losing" its English; it is more plausible to affirm that US society is moving toward more frequent bilingualism.

Whatever the facts, there are political currents that need, in order to exist, to spread the myth that the US is in severe danger of losing its cultural identity (assumed to be a fixed essence) and to provoke tensions over the language question. The two major anti-foreign-language lobbies, English First and US English, are prime examples. They have won several important battles in the past few years and have succeeded in creating ideological polarisation over the question. The June 1998 referendum that in one stroke abolished bilingual education in the public schools of California is a particularly significant event in this regard, but there are more than 20 states and many cities that have passed laws or ordinances prohibiting the use of foreign languages for official acts.

In the wake of civil rights legislation passed under President Johnson, a federal law passed in 1968 authorised the use of federal funds for bilingual programmes created in the different states, provided that the objective of these programmes was to facilitate the transition to English for pupils with a different mother tongue. The Supreme Court confirmed the constitutionality of this principle in 1974. However, the existing legislation was partially eviscerated during the presidency of Ronald Reagan, as a result of well-financed "English Only" campaigns that hammered on a simple message: bilingual education is not only a danger for national identity but also pedagogically unsound. The federal Office of Bilingual Education and Minority Languages Affairs still functions, but since the Reagan era, programmes of English-language immersion without transition may also receive federal funding (see FUCHS, 1990, ch. 24).

In California, the adversaries of bilingual education were successful in drawing attention to an undeniable pedagogical handicap of bilingual education in that state: it had proven impossible to hire enough competent bilingual teachers (not surprising in a state whose system of public education has suffered greatly from loss of taxpayer support). Bilingual education, whatever its intrinsic worth or educational potential, had indeed lost much of its credibility, inciting a significant percentage of Latino voters to oppose it in the June 1998 referendum. It cannot be claimed, then, that educational arguments invoked against bilingual education are totally unfounded, but in practice they function as a thin rhetorical veil to hide another and more worrisome objective of the campaign: to provoke a reaction against Spanish and Spanish-speakers, i.e. to draw borderlines between "good" citizens —full-fledged members of the national community— and those who, because of their insufficient mastery of English, are designated as unworthy of belonging to that community.

Although they have scored some victories recently, English Only militants have not definitively established the rules concerning the use of foreign languages. Federal courts have on several occasions recognised the rights of persons deprived of access to social services because of their imperfect command of English. In any event, the constant arrival of Spanish-speaking immigrants and the growth of Spanish-speaking enclaves in many cities, and the development of dense communication networks linking Latinos in many different contexts, render completely illusory any hopes nourished by English Only militants of eliminating Spanish from the public scene. The question will inevitably have to be addressed in a less confrontational mode at a later time.

It should be noted in passing that one state that has no English Only legislation is Texas, which is clearly conservative in many other respects. In a wide swath of territory along the state's southern border, many people speak both languages, switching back and forth as a matter of routine. This helps to explain why many writers who seek to promote the idea of "hybrid identities" use the border experience as a paradigm for where they see society as a whole evolving (see e.g. SALDÍVAR, 1997).

Does Latinisation imply multiculturalism?

Among the proclaimed defenders of the interests of US Latinos are many partisans of *multiculturalism*. The uncontrollably polysemic character of this term does not contribute to the clarity of debates. The most elementary form of multiculturalist ideology expresses the desire to break with a cultural model seen as dominant and constraining (Anglophone, white, Christian, etc.), imposed on immigrants and other people of "different" origins. The proponents of multiculturalism in this sense aspire to a politics in which particular groups (by national or ethnic origin, religion, gender, sexual orientation, etc.) who seek to express their own interests and aspirations are free to do so: African Americans, Latinos, Chinese and other Asians, women, gays and lesbians, etc.

Opposed to this orientation are those who seek to defend a culture seen indeed as dominant, and justly so, but in danger of losing its dominance: a culture borne by the English language and often defined as well as being based on a certain conception of Christian values, on an acceptance of market forces as the supreme arbiter of social questions, etc. These defenders of the dominant cultural model accuse multiculturalists of seeking to divide and weaken the nation by undermining its founding identity. These debates are well known, largely thanks to the caricatured form they assumed in polemics about "political correctness".

We may take it as a given that the public sphere in the US (to speak here only of one country) is occupied by movements and organisations that openly speak in the name of diverse "communities" of origin (see HOLLINGER, 1999). This is a matter of historical fact that I do not propose either to celebrate or denounce. However, the presence of ethnic discourses and mobilisations in the political sphere does not mean that the US political system can *ipso facto* be designated a multiculturalist one. It is certainly not the case if, by this term, we mean a codified system of rights accorded to different communities of descent (ethnic, "racial", religious, or national groups), on the premise that each group is the bearer of a distinct "culture" or "heritage" that is worthy of being protected and even publicly celebrated. (This definition, which strikes me as being as practical as any other in assigning a clear content to the notion of multiculturalism, is derived from the work of Will Kymlicka (see KYMLICKA, 1995)). The French sociologist Michel Wieviorka makes a useful distinction between "integrated" multiculturalist systems and those which are "fragmented" (*éclatés*), that is, less coherent (WIEVIORKA, 1999). While Canada, Sweden or the Netherlands might provide examples of integrated systems because of coherent bodies of legislation and institutional practices based on the recognition of ethnocultural groups, the US clearly falls into the category of fragmented systems. Although "multiculturalism" is a leitmotif in the discourses of many groups of African Americans, Latinos, Asians, women, gays, etc., it is very infrequent that given instances of the US political system codify collective rights of cultural recognition. One can point to "pockets" of multiculturalism, that is, spaces where demands for recognition of diversity are taken into account with greater success than elsewhere (certain universities, certain municipalities, etc.), but this does not add up to a coherent "model of citizenship" or "model of integration" on a national scale, far from it. On the contrary, the definition of such a model remains, at the national scale, an intensely contested terrain: there is no consensus on the matter. Federal recognition of bilingual education as a legitimate pedagogical method is not, properly speaking, an expression of multiculturalism, because, as we have seen, its main purpose is to assure equal access to education for pupils with limited command of English —not to protect any given minority language or culture (Spanish, Chinese, Vietnamese, etc.). Nor do affirmative action policies represent multiculturalism in any rigorous sense, since their objective is not to protect or promote the cultural expression *per se* of given groups, but to favour the socio-economic interests of these groups by favouring their access to jobs, educational institutions or contracts.

It is no accident, of course, that multicultural citizenship in the US has such a fragmented character. The complex federal architecture of the political system and its tendency to decentralise the treatment of many social problems makes it impossible to speak of a homogeneous policy framework for the integration of given ethnic groups. Nor is there any unified US model for the incorporation of immigrants (see BODY-GENDROT, 1991). There is no national institutional framework in the realm of education, nor any coherent national policy for the management of cultural and linguistic diversity, but rather a patchwork of different policies —or absence of policies— by state, county and city, as well as different ways of interpreting and implementing existing laws.

While one may speak of a dominant model of citizenship in a country like France, it is difficult or impossible to define such a model for the United States. Whatever else one may think of it, the French "republican model of integration" and the norms of *laïcité* continue to provide broad guidelines for the treatment of "communities of descent" on a national scale. Much could be said about the crises and contradictions of the French model, and even the possibility of its dissolution in a foreseeable future, but for the moment it continues to function and has yet to encounter any coherent rival conception. In the US, by contrast, there is no hegemonic model of integration. The polemics over "multiculturalism", often prodigious in their confusion, express in their own way the absence of a consensus over a universally acceptable model.

An ongoing problem with many ordinary conceptions of multiculturalism is that they take it for granted that there are different "cultures" within the nation-state, but never specify what is meant by "a culture" nor by what method distinctions and boundaries can be drawn among different cultures, thereby foreclosing the possibility that they might exist in dynamic interaction and generate new hybrid forms as a matter of course. The boundary question is therefore in many ways a false one, but the US state perpetuates it by bureaucratically defining different ethno-racial groupings to which social actors then often ascribe cultural attributes. David Hollinger has shown convincingly how the ethno-racial "pentagon", as he calls it mockingly (whites, African Americans, Latinos, Native Americans, Asians and Pacific Islanders) functions as a reductive mechanism in drawing supposedly cultural distinctions among groups (HOLLINGER, 1999, 1995). What this conception fails to take into account is that to a large degree, all the groups within the nationally bounded social space of the US share a *common culture*: the commercial culture of capitalism, the mass media, the standardised culture of fast food chains, as well as the mass spectacle culture of sports. Roberto Suro, author of an excellent book-length reportage on Latinos in the US today, asserts that "the American consumer culture penetrated deep into the Latin psyche, informing every appetite and defining new desires" (SURO, 1999, p. 20). He adds: "With TV shows, soldiers, and political ideals, the United States has reached out and touched people across an entire hemisphere. It has gotten back immigrants in return."

Of course, Latino spaces of public expression do exist in certain regions of the country. Some Spanish-language newspapers, such as *La Opinión* of Los Angeles and *El Diario/La Prensa* of New York, are quite influential. There are also a few genuine Latin media empires, such as *Univisión*, *Telemundo* and the Mexican group *Televisa*, whose programmes are available on cable across the continent, and whose viewers constitute a market that is more and more attractive to large corporations. Arlene Dávila's work on Hispanic advertising agencies in New York represents an important contribution to our understanding of how the Latino public is perceived in marketing strategy. (See LAO-MONTES/DÁVILA, 2001.) But one might well ask where, outside of language itself, the cultural difference lies between these organs and networks and those of the Anglo mainstream. It may be that the *telenovelas* broadcast over the Spanish TV channels evoke human situations and passions different from those of analogous productions in English. But can such differences, portrayed on television screens in the context of a common national market, be theorised as manifestations of a distinct culture? Similarly, one could evoke, as evidence of cultural distinctiveness, all the typically Latino consumer products targeted for an "ethnic market", but many of these —food items for example— are available in the restaurants and supermarkets frequented by ethnically diverse publics in many urban areas. These commodities now belong to a growing category of "ethnic" products that interest the Anglo public and end up becoming perfectly run of the mill, as in the case of Italian, Polish, Jewish or Chinese speciality items.

Both the supporters and the detractors of "multiculturalism" agree on what seems to them the obvious idea that several different cultures coexist within the national space. The only disagreement —but it is a serious one— concerns the question of how this diversity should be managed: by imposing a single, dominant (white Anglo) cultural model in the public sphere or by allowing all "cultures" to occupy this sphere with equal opportunity and equal rights of expression. Not only do both sides rest their cases on dubious assumptions, as I have tried to show, but they do so in the name of models (implicit or explicit) for managing ethno-cultural diversity that hardly seem ideal for settling conflicts and promoting social harmony. Furthermore, by dwelling on and fetishising the question of how to manage differences of origin, both sides obscure a serious issue: what to do about the socio-economic inequalities of which disproportionate numbers of Latinos are victims (especially though not exclusively among recent immigrants). Framing the Latino question as quintessentially one of "cultural difference" is a powerful way of obscuring social tensions that arise from the crippling socio-economic insecurity suffered by millions of Latinos in urban *barrios* and no few rural areas across the country.

In other words, I would recommend subsuming the question of the "mode of integration" (or mode of management of cultural and linguistic diversity) under that of the "social model" *tout court*. A model of society that organises the superexploitation of millions of immigrants and their descendants while at the same time chasing many of them into illegality, a model that is unequipped to provide a decent education to large numbers of children in these groups, could within a few years provoke strong resistance which could not only take the form of socio-economic demands and struggles against workplace and linguistic discrimination, but could also spill over into more narrowly ethnicised concerns. As we shall see further on, the forms of political mobilisation common to Latinos invoke ethnic references in a rather moderate way in the US context. However, if there is one sure way to push Latinos to withdraw into more ingrown identity politics, it is by allowing the effects of neoliberal economics to continue without remedy.

Inequalities and their political implications

Is there really such a thing as a Latino collectivity? The "Hispanics" who make up an official category of the national census spring from many different national origins and cover the entire gamut of social conditions. What is there in common, aside possibly from the use of Spanish, between a Cuban entrepreneur in Miami and a Mexican day labourer in Los Angeles? Research shows as well that within each national group there is a growing social polarisation: what is there in common between the Puerto Rican single mother in the Bronx and the

Puerto Rican lawyer in Miami? Rather than a "Hispanic condition" (STAVANS, 1995), it seems more fitting to recognise a multiplicity of conditions.

Nonetheless, many social-science studies are based precisely on the notion that there is a "Hispanic condition", just as one might refer to a "black condition", ignoring the wide gulf between the lifestyle of an African-American business executive and that of an unemployed ghetto dweller. Why? There is no secret: even social scientists are strongly influenced by the ethnically-based thinking in which the society as a whole is submerged. They prefer to overlook the socio-economic cleavages *within* given populations in order to bring out the inequalities of which these groups are seen as *collective* victims. Once this logic is accepted, it is impossible to deny that Latinos, taken as a whole, are confronted with major problems of socio-economic integration, as the following figures demonstrate:

—There is a significant, durable and worsening income differential between Latinos and non-Latinos. In 1991, the median income for a Puerto Rican household was measured at $16,169; for a Mexican household, $22,439; as compared to $29,943 for the rest of the population (CORDERO GUZMÁN, 1998, p. 83).
—Latinos have a higher rate of employment than whites. In July 1992, 11.9 per cent of the adult Latino population was without work; the same was true of 14.6 per cent of adult Afro-Americans and 6.7 per cent of whites (PÉREZ/SALAZAR, 1998, p. 49).
—In 1990, 28.7 per cent of all Latinos —including 40.4 per cent of Latino children!— were classified as poor (PÉREZ/SALAZAR, 1998, p. 51). By comparison, in the same period, 37.2 per cent of African-Americans and 11.3 per cent of whites were classified as poor.
—In 1992, one white person out of eight had no form of medical insurance; the same was true for one African-American out of five and one Latino out of three (PÉREZ/SALAZAR, 1998, p. 51).
—As a group, Latinos make up the least educated sector of the US population (PÉREZ/SALAZAR, 1998, p. 48-49). In 1991, only 51.3 per cent of Latinos of over 25 years of age had finished four years of secondary education, as against 80.5 per cent of the "non-Hispanic" population. Only 10 per cent of Latinos over 25 had finished four years of higher education.
—Latinos as a whole suffer from very high dropout rates. Currently about 40 per cent of Latinos registered in a secondary school interrupt their studies before graduation. In 1990, 37.7 per cent

of Latinos between ages 18 and 24 had left secondary school without a diploma, as against only 15.1 per cent of blacks and 13.5 per cent of whites.

—Latinos are under-represented in the liberal professions and in executive positions in private enterprise (PÉREZ/SALAZAR, 1998, p. 49). According to figures for the year 1988, 25.6 per cent of whites in the active population were classified as managers or professionals, as opposed to only 15.4 per cent of blacks and 13.2 per cent of Latinos. Jobs classified as involving "material production" (i.e. factory workers) were held in 1988 by 14 per cent of active whites, 22.9 per cent of active blacks and 23.9 per cent of active Latinos. Such low-skilled industrial jobs, as is well known, are in the process of disappearing. In the future, the best-paid jobs in industry will require much greater levels of qualification, which many Latinos will lack because of low educational attainments.

The implications of these figures for the socio-economic integration of Latinos are clearly worrying. Groups speaking in the name of Latino interests naturally use them as arguments in their plea for more equal opportunity. The national absence of consensus concerning the model of integration encounters here one of its most direct expressions: while most Latino movements call for conserving ethnically-targeted measures (*affirmative action*) to hasten collective Latino socio-economic integration, nearly all conservatives —including no small number of Latinos— firmly oppose such measures.

Affirmative action, as is well known, is a "wedge" issue that can easily be used to polarise public opinion. That is why a conservative intellectual such as Peter Skerry has made it a point to suggest, in his work on Mexican-Americans, that this group has collectively wandered into an approach to socio-economics which draws too much inspiration from the African-American experience (SKERRY, 1993). According to this author, the classic model of integration —that pursued by white European immigrants at the turn of the twentieth century— is an objective that Mexicans could have adopted had their political leaders not misguided them into a "racial" mode of mobilisation. Skerry's apparent universalist common sense is betrayed by his very tendentious reading of history, for although he feigns not to remember, the daily experience of Mexicans in the southwest US was for a long time made up of discrimination and socio-economic exclusion by Anglos, in a quasi-colonial mode. It was not by some act of bad faith, but rather as a result of the bitter experience of victimisation, that the Chicano movement, in the mid to late 60s, drew inspiration not only from the civil rights movement, but also from the black power movement.

The double radicalism —social and ethnic— of the Chicano movement is today a fading memory. The most influential Latino lobbying groups are resolutely reformist and call for stronger social policies for *all* categories of the population while continuing to articulate the ethnic reference in a moderate mode. However, in the absence of a coherent national policy to combat socio-economic exclusion regardless of the victims' origins, it seems logical and politically expedient for Latino organisations to continue to call not only for universalist solutions but *also* for remedies targeted at Latinos in particular.

Integration via the *barrios*?

Although the socio-economic indices cited above suggest a generally troubling situation for Latinos, all figures do not point in this direction. Another frequently quoted indicator of negative social welfare is the percentage of single-parent households. Statistics on this question project the image of a Latino population relatively secure in its ability to reproduce nuclear families. In 1990, 19.3 per cent of all Anglo homes and 23.8 per cent of Latino homes were headed by single parents, as opposed to an astronomical 58 per cent of African-American families (PÉREZ/SALAZAR, 1998, p. 51-52). In the Latino category, however, there were notable differences among groups by national origin: 19.1 per cent of Mexican homes and 19.4 per cent of Cuban homes were headed by single parents as compared to 43.3 per cent of Puerto Rican homes. One partial conclusion that could be drawn from these figures is that the disastrous effects of ghettoisation on family life, as depicted by sociologist William J. Wilson in the case of black ghettos (WILSON, 1987), are manifested to a much lesser degree in poor Mexican urban areas (see MOORE/PANDERHUGHES, 1993).

One of the reasons that the social fabric in Latino *barrios* is said to be more solid than in black ghettos is that Latinos have succeeded in creating enclaves of ethnic commerce. One might therefore be led to think that Latinos, armed with the resources of discipline and family and community solidarity, are relatively well placed to confront the difficulties of socio-economic integration in spite of the hardships they often face at first. However, even when given groups of immigrants display an exceptional capacity for economic integration they are not necessarily in a position to guarantee the successful integration of their children. Quoting studies by sociologist Alejandro Portes (PORTES/

ZHOU, 1993; see also PORTES, 1996), Suro notes that "the chances for downward mobility are greatest for second-generation youth who live in close proximity to American minorities who are poor to start with and who themselves are victims of ethnic or racial discrimination" (SURO, 1999, p. 51). The chances for advancement for these youth are further diminished by an ethnic division of labour that often reserves for Latinos the most poorly paid jobs (DAVIS, 2000, ch. 9), and by the critical situation of US cities, which are more and more deprived of fiscal resources by the federal government (DAVIS, 2000, ch. 11).

I do not claim, in these few pages, to capture the "essence" of social dynamics in Latino *barrios*, but it is clear from even casual reading on this subject that many such areas are zones of exclusion at least as much as they are spaces of integration into US society. Suro warns that "the new Latino settlements will still be new and tender and disconnected for decades to come" (SURO, 1999, p. 208). If the immense mass of young people, either immigrants themselves or children of immigrants, could acquire adequate education for finding a place in the new service economy —a daring hypothesis at this point— then there might be some hope for their successful integration, all cultural issues aside. However, if no energetic public policy is elaborated to favour their integration, then the danger of social explosions will be great, along with the probability of new flareups of xenophobia. Already the signs of tension are alarming. Mike Davis documents in great detail the tendency for the residents of some affluent, white neighbourhoods in California to seal themselves off from Latinos (he calls this phenomenon "the third border") and designate them, in classic scapegoat fashion, as a malevolent "brown peril" responsible for criminal violence and depriving native-born Americans of jobs (DAVIS, 2000, chs. 6, 7). The dynamics of everyday life that can lead in the direction of this "apartheid scenario" are magnificently described by T. C. Boyle in his novel *The Tortilla Curtain* (1995).

The diversity of the Latino political "bloc"

In a system that recognises and even fabricates "communities of descent", Latinos are perceived and often perceive themselves as an ethnic bloc despite, as we have seen, the immense diversity of social conditions and political horizons of Latino populations. Wherever a large Latino population may be found, media commentators and scholars track the "Hispanic vote" and the signs of emergence of an ethnic elite taken to be representative of the "community". Latinos as a group are often described by political commentators as a "sleeping giant" in the process of awaking from its slumber; that is, a huge mass of voters or potential voters whose collective influence, already considerable, can only grow further in the coming decades (see DESIPIO, 1996, for an exceptionally rigorous and lucid approach to this question). Since they are geographically concentrated in a few, very populous states, they exercise a particularly great influence in presidential elections. Any serious presidential candidate must address specific messages to Latinos, using their best Spanish if possible. There are currently 20 Latino Representatives in Congress (all Democrats but three, including two Cubans from Miami). Since the 1980s, several Latinos have occupied important positions in the federal government. One man who symbolises the new Latino political elite is Henry Cisneros, elected first Latino mayor of San Antonio in 1981, who briefly served as Clinton's Secretary of Housing and Urban Development (1993-1995) before being overtaken by legal problems. He then became president of the large media group *Univisión*.

Further understanding of the nature of Latinos' incorporation into the political system would require examining the little-explored role of lobbying groups such as the National Council of La Raza, LULAC (League of Latin American Citizens), and a few others which exercise an important influence in defining strategic options. The Congressional Hispanic Caucus would also deserve attention in this light.

But to what extent can these groups and individuals bring about policy decisions that favour the integration of those millions of Latinos —recent or not-so-recent immigrants or children of immigrants— who experience serious socio-economic difficulties? The truth is that they have few means and little margin for manoeuvre to carry out their programme. The experience of African Americans, who have elected mayors to a large number of big cities since the 1960s and hold 40 seats in Congress, clearly shows that political influence —at the local, state or even at the federal level— can remain without any noticeable effect on the condition of the "truly disadvantaged". Latino legislators in Congress have undergone a series of severe defeats in recent years, in particular on questions of social services and education (*NEW YORK TIMES*, 1997).

True enough, in certain situations Latinos can indeed coalesce into a unified electoral force. For example, in angry opposition to the anti-immigrant campaign with strong racist overtones waged by former California governor Pete Wilson, the "sleeping giant" began to stir and succeeded in causing Wilson's divisive strategy to backfire: not only was the ballot initiative Proposition 187 (1994) found by federal courts to be unconstitutional in most of its particulars, but the anti-Hispanic backlash nourished by the campaign in favour of the ballot initiative was countered by an unprecedented wave of Latino political participation, including large numbers of naturalisations and registrations of new voters, the radicalisation of a broad sector of young people of Mexican origin, and finally the defeat of the Republican candidate (Wilson's would-be successor) in the 1998 gubernatorial elections, thanks in great part to this burst of voter mobilisation.

Nonetheless, the Latino "bloc" that many expect or hope to see emerge is more fragmented than is often believed. The Latino collective reference, like all other ethnic appeals, is by definition a broad interpellation, a "catchall" figure of rhetoric that can be mobilised to all sorts of political ends. It sometimes takes the form of a particularist discourse through which more universalistic aims are articulated, but even when accompanied by a universalist vision of social justice, it can still remain subject to instrumentalisation by self-promoting elites. Sociologist Agustín Lao-Montes proposes a typology of five "ideologies of Latin power", which he defines as five analytically distinct orientations that tend in reality to mix together: 1) "ethnic Keynesianism", 2) "Latino populism", 3) Latino neo-conservatism, 4) Latin American radical vanguardism and 5) radical democracy (LAO-MONTES/DÁVILA, 2001, pp. 133-140).

For reasons of space, these various perspectives cannot be developed in detail here. I will simply note that according to Lao-Montes, one of these types, "ethnic Keynesianism", has long functioned as a "dominant ideology" of Latino access to power. This orientation is based on a belief in the capacity of the state to resolve problems of socio-economic inequality that concern Latinos, via the distribution of public goods.

Although Lao's typology does not claim to be exhaustive, it does show that the diversity of political perspectives among Latinos renders impossible any prophecy as to Latinos' overall impact in national political life. From the mini-renaissance of the labour movement on the west coast, which owes much to the energies of Latino activists struggling to fight their way out of the condition of working poor (see NACLA, 1996; DAVIS, 2000, ch. 15), some might be tempted to extrapolate that there is something naturally "progressive" about Latino political activity, but no one kind of political or movement-oriented involvement is necessarily emblematic: alongside these labour activists one also finds local political leaders who stir up divisions between Latinos and blacks, Latino businessmen who use the language of Latino identity to struggle for "their fair share" of municipal contracts, and no small number of conservative voters who are seduced by Republicans' frequent references to "family values" and assimilate these to Latin traditions.

The idea that Latinos will necessarily contribute to the formation of a left-wing pole in US politics springs, then, more from wishful thinking than from cold analysis. The "Hispanic vote" is indeed preponderantly Democratic, with the obvious exception of the Cuban population in southern Florida, but it must also be taken into account that in the Clinton era, even more then earlier times, the social and economic policies of the Democratic Party have become hardly distinguishable from those of the Republicans: witness for example Clinton's 1994 Crime Bill, the momentous welfare reform initiated in 1996, the considerable reinforcement of the Border Patrol in recent years, and the Clinton administration's ardent attachment to eliminating the federal budget deficit (earlier an exclusively Republican obsession). Under these circumstances, it cannot be ruled out that many voters might have trouble making a clear choice. Since the New Deal era, Democrats have successfully presented themselves as the "natural" party of ethnic minorities and immigrants, but the Republicans have begun to demonstrate, during their 2000 national convention for example, that they too can adopt the rhetoric of the "big tent" to which all ethnic groups are welcome. And even if there is more show than substance to this new rhetoric of inclusion, there are in some areas, including George W. Bush's home state of Texas for example, strong nuclei of conservative Latinos who can legitimately hope to sway a Latin majority to their side.

In short, no one can predict with certainty the long-term political impact of the massive entry of Latinos into the exercise of US citizenship. The only prediction I would hazard takes the form of an alternative: if the system does not open up toward Latinos in the socio-economic margins of society, as well as to other excluded citizens and non-citizens, providing them with paths toward education, skills and employment, the country may well be headed toward a new era of social explosions in the urban areas of heavy Latino concentration. The groups pushed into the margins by a run-down educational system and by subsistence wages cannot remain content forever with the "little bit more" that recent immigrants find on the northern side of the border (cf. MONSIVÁIS, 1995). Demands for increased material welfare and greater political participation are inevitable; rising frustration is likely if no decisive action is taken to change the shape of the US social model. It is of course beyond the scope of this paper (and beyond the capacity of its author) to define with any precision the array of social forces that could lead toward such change.

Assigning culture to its place

I wish to conclude by reiterating, with some qualifications, the central thesis of this paper, i.e., that the cultural and linguistic cast frequently given to the theme of Latinisation may serve as a decoy that diverts attention from the socio-economic circumstances that render particularly difficult the integration of many Latinos into US society. This is not, of course, to deny that cultural issues may have a logic of their own and may thus call for treatment that goes beyond republican (small "r") conceptions of integration through the reinforcement of civil, political and social rights. Although I suggest above —and still firmly maintain— that much of what is presented as Latin "difference" is reduced all too easily to products on a market where exoticism is a good sales argument, there are aspects of the incorporation of Latinos into US society that bring difference to the heart of relations between themselves and the Anglo population. The integration of Latinos into US society is crucially a matter of education, employment, wages, civil rights, political participation, but it is also, undeniably, a question of culture. A good case in point would be the issue of the aesthetics of house decoration: as Mike Davis relates in his recent book, some Anglo neighbourhoods in California object to the "exotic" colours chosen by Latinos when they paint their homes. It may be true, as Davis suggests, that Latinos have a different approach from Anglos to living in cities. He writes:

> In the most fundamental sense, the Latinos are struggling to reconfigure the "cold" frozen geometries of the old spatial order to accommodate a "hotter", more exuberant urbanism... [The] social reproduction of latinidad, however defined, presupposes a rich proliferation of public space. The most intense and creative convergence of Ibero-Mediterranean and Meso-American cultures is precisely their shared conviction that civilised sociality is constituted in the daily intercourse of the plaza and mercado... (DAVIS, 2000, p. 54).

Some might argue that Davis is guilty here of attributing an "essence" to *latinidad* rather than seeing it as a malleable form to which various contents can be associated depending on historical circumstance. Others might object that he idealises a certain conception of urban sociality and seeks to invest Latinos with an historical mission to realise it. And yet it seems undeniable that a significant *perception* exists that Latinos have a different way of occupying urban space and that their increasing presence in US cities could raise the question of whether that conception of space can prevail over the dominant one.

The question in one sense appears systemic, that is, bound up with the dynamics of capitalist organisation of urban space, but it is also undeniably cultural, pointing to areas of choice and spaces of imagination within that system (or even, as Davis seems to suggest, beyond it).

It is nonetheless my conviction that an exaggerated tendency exists to "culturalise" the question of Latinisation by reducing it to matters of language, music, food and —why not?— urban life styles. To insist only on the cultural is to insist on "diversity", on the irreducible difference of *latinidad*, and thereby to feed into the discourses of differentialism that thrive on showing how inassimilable Latinos are. The antidote to such discourses can only be the insistence on rights of material well-being and political participation to which all citizens, regardless of origin and "culture", should be entitled. This is a matter of principle, which I articulate in full knowledge of how far removed the US political system is from a republican order in which citizens' rights can be articulated in a non-differentialist way.

We thus return, in conclusion, to the question of what sort of nation the United States really is. I find useful here the oxymoronic formula proposed by Denis Lacorne when he says that the US is an "ethno-civic" nation, "ethnic by exclusion and civic by inclusion" (LACORNE, 1997, p. 15). While it may be true that this dialectic is not only unresolved but irresolvable, that does not prevent particular citizens from taking a stand closer to one ideal or the other. However, the real question, for the United States, is not whether to opt for one model to the exclusion of the other, but to determine to what degree the principles of a civic nation can channel and limit the differentialist impulses of the ethnic nation. It may well be that some version of official "multiculturalism" may be the only politically possible formula for attaining this goal in the US, given its history, but one can formulate the hope that it would be, in Lacorne's words, a "controlled", "republicanised" multiculturalism rather than a system conceived to consecrate supposedly irreducible differences among categories of citizens by origin. In this respect, I would suggest that the progressive facet of political Latinisation offers some hopeful signs. The appeals articulated by social and political actors in the name of a democratic *latinidad* take much more often the form of "ethnic formulations of social demands" (CONSTANT, 2000) than of purely differentialist discourses leading in a separatist direction. And even these "ethnic formulations" are attenuated by simultaneous appeals for new rights in the name of citizens of all origins. However, the vectors of this democratic *latinidad* are certainly not in a position to decide by themselves which way the wind will blow. The differentialist and sometimes even segregationist currents we have mentioned here may also succeed in stirring up harsher ethnic responses, a new radical *chicanismo* for example. Beyond this point, only close observation of social and political dynamics can help us better understand where the United States and its burgeoning Latino population are heading. The content and ultimate significance of Latinisation remain open.

References

BARTH, F. (1969): *Ethnic Groups and Boundaries: The Social Organisation of Cultural Differences*. Allen & Unwin/Forgalet, London and Oslo.
BODY-GENDROT, S. (1991): *Les États-Unis et leurs immigrants: des modes d'insertion variés*. La Documentation française, Paris.
BOYLE, T. C. (1995) *The Tortilla Curtain*, Viking, New York.
COHEN, J. (1999): "Consensus introuvable à Porto-Rico", *Le Monde diplomatique*, April.
CONSTANT, F. (2000): *Le Multiculturalisme*. Flammarion, Paris.
CORDERO GUZMÁN, H. R. (1998): "The Structure of Inequality and the Status of Puerto Rican Youth in the United States". In *Latinos and Education: A Critical Reader*, ed. A. Darder, R. Torres and H. Gutiérrez. Routledge, New York/London.
CRAWFORD, J. W. (n.d.) "Demographic Change and Language", Language Policy Web Site, http:/ourworld.compuserve.com/homepages/jwcrawford/.
DAVIS, M. (1999): "Magical Urbanism: Latinos Reinvent the US Big City", *New Left Review* 234, March-April.
DAVIS, M. (2000): *Magical Urbanism: Latinos Reinvent the US City*. Verso, London/New York.
DESIPIO, L. (1996): *Counting on the Latino Vote: Latinos as a New Electorate*. University of Virginia Press, Charlottesville, VA.
FUCHS, L. H. (1990): *The American Kaleidoscope: Race, Ethnicity and the Civic Culture*. Wesleyan University Press, Middletown, CT.
GÓMEZ-PEÑA, G. (1993): "From Art-Mageddon to Gringostroika", *Warrior for Gringostroika: Essays, Performance Texts and Poetry*. Graywolf Press, Saint Paul.
GUTIÉRREZ, D. G. (1998): "Ethnic Mexicans and the Transformation of 'American' Social Space: Reflections on Recent History". In *Crossings: Mexican Immigration in Interdisciplinary Perspectives*, ed. M. Suárez-Orozco. Harvard University Press/David Rockefeller Center for Latin American Studies, Cambridge, Mass./London.
HOLLINGER, D. C. (1995): *Post-Ethnic America: Beyond Multiculturalism*. Basic Books, New York.
HOLLINGER, D. C. (1999): "National Culture and Communities of Descent". In *Diversity and its Discontents: Cultural Conflict and Common Ground in Contemporary American Society*, ed. Neil J. Smelser and Jeffrey C. Alexander. Princeton University Press, Princeton, NJ.

KYMLICKA, W. (1995): *Multicultural Citizenship*. Oxford University Press, Oxford.
LACORNE, D. (1997): *La Crise de l'identité américaine*. Fayard, Paris.
LAO-MONTES, A.; DÁVILA, A. (eds.) (2001) *Mambo Montage: The Latinization of New York City*. Columbia University Press, Columbia.
MONSIVÁIS, C. (1995): "Dreaming of Utopia", *NACLA Report on the Americas*, Vol. 29, No. 3.
MOORE, J.; PANDERHUGHES, R. (eds.) (1993): *In the Barrios: Latinos and the Underclass Debate*. Russell Sage Foundation, New York .
NACLA (1996): "On the Line: Latinos on Labour's Cutting Edge", *NACLA Report on the Americas*, Vol. 30, No. 3.
NEW YORK TIMES (1997): "For Hispanic Lawmakers, Time to Take the Offensive", 25 August.
PÉREZ, S. M.; SALAZAR, D. (1998): "Economic, Labour Force and Social Implications of Latino Educational and Population Trends". In *Latinos and Education: A Critical Reader*, ed. A. Darder, R. Torres and H. Gutiérrez. Routledge, London.
PORTES, A. (1996): *The New Second Generation*, Russell Sage Foundation, New York.
PORTES, A.; ZHOU, M. (1993): "The New Second Generation: Segmented Assimilation and Its Variants", *Annals of the American Academy of Political and Social Sciences*, November.
SALDÍVAR, J. D. (1997): *Border Matters: Remapping American Cultural Studies*, University of California Press, Berkeley, CA.
SKERRY, P. (1993): *Mexican Americans: The Ambivalent Minority*. Harvard University Press, Cambridge, Mass./London.
STAVANS, I. (1995): *The Hispanic Condition: Reflections on Culture and Identity in America*. Harper-Collins, New York.
SUÁREZ-OROZCO, M. (1998): "Crossings: Mexican Immigration in Interdisciplinary Perspectives", introduction to the book of the same title, Harvard University Press/David Rockefeller Center for Latin American Studies, Cambridge, Mass./London.
SURO, R. (1999): *Strangers Among Us: Latin Lives in the Changing America*. Vintage, New York.
US CENSUS BUREAU (1999): Population Estimates Programme, Population Division, US Census Bureau, Washington, D.C., figures published on Internet on October 29, 1999 [http://www.census.gov]
US CENSUS BUREAU (1995): *Population Projections of the United States by Age, Sex, Race and Hispanic Origins, 1995 to 2050*, Washington, D.C., Government Printing Office,
WIEVIORKA, M. (1999): "Le multiculturalisme: solution, ou formulation d'un problème?" In *Immigration et intégration, l'état des savoirs*, ed. Philippe Dewitte. La Découverte, Paris.
WILSON, W. J. (1987): *The Truly Disadvantaged: The Inner City, the Underclass and Public Policy*. University of Chicago Press, Chicago.

Western Europe in the Urban Gap Between Mobility and Migration Flows

Barbara Verlic Christensen

Introduction: main theses on contemporary migration research

After ten years of transitional changes we see former socialist societies opening up their borders and institutions. The extent of such opening up threatens their social cohesion: it is marked by loose organisation, floating institutions, involving mobility and the migration of different ethnic groups. This process is not being sufficiently recorded. It has been described as the "leap in the dark" of new movements of people within and across borders; away from the periphery into the core developed countries and towards mostly urban destinations. Meanwhile, previously open societies, specifically Western European ones, are closing up and (bureaucratically) struggling to regulate the new migratory flows. The anachronistic European paradigm, as one obstacle to mobility, requires the cultural, local integration of new residents. This explicit demand seems to disguise the demand for cultural assimilation.

In the same vein, the process of social and cultural integration is being contradicted by closed and discriminatory local practices of the dominant society. Increased competition for jobs and educational opportunities is dislocating the borders of nation-states. It is changing the emphasis from regional and local areas to global ones. Such a disjunction prompts the local and institutional systems to make adjustments, and to protect and defend national interests in order to avoid any unmanageable, unwanted social changes. The consequences are division of employment within urban centres and the segregation of ethnic groups. Increased mobility and ethnic migration do limit and redefine the privileges of the local population in terms of welfare policies, access to education, available employment opportunities and housing. Migration and new mobility do not necessarily represent social promotion as was the case before: often, migrants are hooked into social dependency on the state and/or the family. Finally, ethnic groups increasingly resist the acculturation processes. People within mobility flows are seeking to be integrated into global labour markets, but at the same time they are burdened by and wrapped up within national local entities.

Newcomers often find themselves in the stigmatised and legally void social spaces of nation-states. They are very often socially excluded in the new society, while uprooted from the previous one. This promotes polarisation within the urban structure of Europe. Ethnic migrants stress that integration is a two-way process and involves dialogue, not a monologue: it has two parties, not one actor. The basic demand for integration is a set of forms and actions, presented by local authorities, which are very difficult or even impossible to realise in practice, especially when the migrants no longer have a credible chance of getting employment or an education. The expected and requested social integration of ethnic residents thus does not possess the same legitimisation, since it does not promote the social prosperity of migrants. The request for integration does seem to be necessary to obtain and preserve national cohesion and the process of cultural socialisation. It is estimated as a necessary precondition for adequate development of the sovereignty of the nation-state and preservation of its cultural identity.

This paper presents selected fragments of the ongoing research into ethnicity, migration and the problems of social integration in Scandinavia. Aspects of these phenomena threaten the social cohesion of a United Europe. In the first part, the more general processes and characteristics of the issue are noted. They introduce the broader social and economic background, without which it is difficult to analyse the increasing problems of institutional discrimination, even racism, which we have recently been witnessing in both Western Europe and the former socialist countries. At this point, the analysis of individual cases and data gathered in formal organisations, mostly in Denmark or Sweden, are presented. Finally, some preliminary results and a thesis are formulated. These require critical testing and remain open to further discussion.

The subject and approach used

The lack of new social ideas and policies in the process of European unification results in the exclusion and/or marginalisation of certain groups. My intention is to present the problems of migrants in the EU, specifically in Scandinavia and Denmark. "Marginalisation" of migrants is defined as a lack of control over formal resources that would enable the groups to accommodate, integrate or assimilate within the new environment. In addition, it points to the neglect of ethnic and individual resources for integration itself. Within this ethno-methodological approach (GARFINKEL, 1967), I have carried out an analysis of different, yet structured, personal perceptions of immigrants' own experiences. This approach has also captured some of the emotional reactions to the obstacles to successful integration. Typical patterns emerged and were then tested or confronted with the experiences of the executives in those organisations that promote the social integration of new residents.

The genesis of a social framework for migration in Scandinavia

The unification of Europe has led to progress within the economic domain, realising three main goals and freedoms: free flows of capital, services and goods. The fourth freedom is mobility and migration of the labour force. However, this last provokes tensions and conflicts, and opens the door to xenophobic debates between national entities and certain local inhabitants. The comprehensive image of European society is in question. Consequently, the social and democratic processes of unification are being delayed and social quality is deteriorating. The economic unification of EU countries in progress has produced an asymmetry between the economic determination of everyday lives of citizens, and their social quality (BECK et al., 1997). This asymmetry is nicely encapsulated in the sentiment: "We wanted a labour force, but instead, we got people!"

The evolution of social welfare policies in different Member States did not dynamically follow economic change. The term "social quality" concerns issues of social participation, integration, social security and solidarity, social cohesion and citizens' empowerment. Within these, more specific topics are put forward, such as unemployment (security of income), social exclusion and poverty, access to education and career flexibility, access to active use of modern technologies, information, and political rights. These changes within national societies and the new phenomenon of unification/globalisation as it impacts on social groups all affect the culture and social structure of European populations.

First, the phenomena of modern migration and increased mobility come, in the context of European experiences, as a shock. Since the selective and controlled guest-worker immigration of the 1960s, everything has gone wrong and was ill-predicted (MEDVED, 1998: 29,

51: non-integrational, rotation immigration model). The temporarily settled, unskilled "labour force" in low-paid industrial jobs postponed the trickle-down return scenario. It is estimated that 30-50 % of guest workers actually stayed in the new country. More recently, the ethnic diversity of urban Europe has increased due to flows of refugees and ethnic family formation/reunification. The integration of the second and third ethnic generations has further fostered a distinctive ethnic niche within the European population (KING, 1993).

Second is the fact that these flows are specifically redesigning major cities and urban areas in general. European cities are increasingly focusing on the phenomenon of social division, involving the ethnic duality of urban spaces, fragmentation of urban structures and development perspectives, urban poverty traps, and social polarisation. Recently, crime and conflicts have increased. These phenomena represent a paradox in the endeavour to create equality, and peaceful development of the EU, not to mention social democracy (BECK et al., 1997; CLARK, 1998).

The hope that urban Europe will avoid the negative experiences of the USA is in some danger. The fear of repeating ethnic/class segregation, ethnic tensions, racism, etc. highlights the need to address migration as a priority (ANDERSSON, 1998). Nation-states and the European Community seem to be creating a new fortress that will change democratic values, the meaning of human rights and social quality —and could kill European tradition and cohesion (MASTNAK, 1998). These issues reflect the growing inequalities eroding the long held value of equal social standards and equality itself. They jeopardise the development of a social equilibrium between economic and social issues.

Comparative modesty in economic growth has allowed Nordic countries to sustain traditional local production, a reasonable development risk and the ecological balance. Slower and less flexible European markets have required higher co-operation and mutual agreement (for example the historical Scandinavian compromise between the government and employers) in achieving a social welfare system. This then creates a large and complex organisation in support of public sector services. The social democratic tradition has been marked by local democracy and the decentralisation of decision-making. Government planning has played an important part by increasing the removing of elites from local democracy. All this has been achieved at the price of very high taxes on the one hand, but with secure, prosperous and peaceful social development on the other. These achievements are perceived to be in danger since cultural and ethnic diversity persist, as do rising unemployment rates.

Finally, none of the ideas or policies applied in the social and economic integration of ethnic migrants are really working adequately —to resolve the increasing number of new problems people experience in everyday life (ANDERSSON, 1998). Analyses incorporating everyday perspectives and the experiences of social groups are needed, along with a search for new ideas which should be promoted by Brussels to overcome the "paper designed recommendations", without any firm legal responsibility. The main obstacles in these communications between Member States and EU Commissions are the necessary consensuses upon each issue and the other differences in perspectives at the regional, local or national levels. Democracy and social quality (protection) are the losers in this EU political game (BECK et al. 1997).

Over the last 10-15 years, migration within the EU and, in particular, from third countries has increased the xenophobic reactions of local and national communities. Still, migration and mobility across all borders is increasing and seems irreversible as well. The mobility of people is a precondition for globalisation (KING, 1993). Dominance of the economy (asymmetry) at this point promotes it. The lack of social security and suitable life prospects for a growing number of people and nations are creating the basis for the self-protective, discriminatory mechanisms used in the everyday practices of local organisations (immigration offices, social centres etc.). We talk about institutional discrimination resulting from the way legal systems and norms are applied to deal with the new ethnic problems.

At this point, my research examined the so-called "Scandinavian integration model" from two perspectives. It started from an analysis of individual cases (63 qualitative interviews), and, secondly, related those experiences to the practice of such organisations as the Immigration Office, the Refugee Council, social centres, and refugee associations. The aim was to outline the characteristic patterns of experiences and practices which are repeated in many cases, and therefore typical. As for the difference between the objective normative studies and statistical analyses, it shows the subjective perspectives related and compared to the norms of institutional practices. The goal then is to evaluate the validity and efficiency of the proposed Social Integration Model with respect to the obstacles highlighted by an individual's experience.

The abovementioned structure focused on the basic preconditions for a migrant to be able to sustain himself and, consequently, to integrate socially: recognition of qualifications and education obtained in different countries, access to education within the new country, access to adequate training for new language requirements, employment possibilities, housing and social/family security. There are generally three main ways to immigrate or to be mobile within the EU: employment, family reunification and asylum. Scandinavian countries have open, liberal mobility established for their citizens. Preferential and privileged criteria are used for citizens of the EU, while very tight standards are applied to residents of third countries (MEDVED, 1998). Nevertheless, there is increasing evidence of illegal migration flows coming from the European periphery and aimed at the developed regions of Europe.

The number of new residents in the EU is increasing sharply due to rights obtained for family reunification. They receive, when legal residency status is achieved, basic social security. The latest flows of refugees are only adding to those numbers. Unlike traditional migrations and those of the 1960s, this massive flow is unexpected, unwelcome and uncontrolled. They are the result of accumulated and unresolved problems in different parts of the world, where international regulations or interventions are inefficient. People are simply being forced to take their chances by exchanging one set of problems for another in the hope that they can resolve the former more efficiently (CHRISTENSEN, 1997).

The essential cause of resistance to migration flows is the persistent unemployment problem and ever stronger social insecurity within EU countries (BECK *et al.*, 1997; BERRY, 1995). Whatever the motivation of new residents to move, the common denominator of their expectations is a search for a new social identity. The concept of social integration in Scandinavian countries represents an idealistic goal: after the phase of accommodation in the new country, new residents are expected to actively participate in society and enjoy equal rights and opportunities compared to the domestic population (MEDVED, 1998; DUNN, 1998).

The obstacles to doing this do not reside in legislation or declarations as such, but are rather a consequence of their practical implementation. On the other side, migrants seem to resist cultural assimilation (ANDERSSON, 1998; BONACHICH/LIGHT, 1988). Cultural and ethnic identity is very often the only identity they have left, since many of them have experienced the loss of citizenship, work, family, and social security. In many cases, new residents have no recognised previously obtained qualifications in the new society.

The integration process required somehow seems to conceal an expectation to assimilate. A representative of Bosnian refugees in Sweden shocked the public by expressing on the radio the following resistance to assimilation: "we here are subjected to ethnic cleansing with different methods" (June, 1994). The statement referred to the requirement that divergent ethnic groups should accept the new culture, and its effect on families which were scattered around villages of the North. Newcomers were expected to learn a new language, requalify, forget most of their own culture and experiences —in a way which they saw as paternalistic.

From the immigrants' perspective, this meant the loss of control over their own ethnic or class resources. Thus, the ethnic group lost autonomy and individuals the opportunity of choice. On the other hand, the receiving society gained power and responsibility. When and if the results are not adequate, frustrations are found on both sides. They open a political debate, raise prejudices, justify discrimination and finally, criminalise the victims.

The search for a new social identity as a two-way process

In the 1990s, some 11 million new residents were registered in Europe, but estimates give a figure two to three times higher, counting potential candidates and illegal immigrants. Presently, refugees are the largest source of new residents, and are uncontrolled and unpredicted from the point of view of labour market needs and national policies. There are 40 million refugees registered in the world, while about 100 million are actually in that position as estimated. Integration requires not only the adaptation of immigrants, but an open and tolerant receiving social environment as well. There is a missing link between both sides: the role of government interventions in the existing forms of integration models are insufficient.

The Scandinavian model of integration is marked by typical patterns of experiences, which are at variance with the very idealistic resolutions. The latter promise equality in social standards and equal treatment before the law, while the experiences reveal the obstacles to achieving it. Denmark and Sweden, where most data were analysed, are both highly regulated countries with complex welfare systems. The integration model is based on the classical theory of ethnic assimilation (PARK/BURGESS/MCKENZIE, 1925; DUNN, 1998). A high level of organisation is provided for the first phase of integration, like housing (often a camp!), medical assistance and teaching programmes. Fundamental organisation in the second phase is devolved to local communities, firms and families. Here the problems begin. Based on the experiences of immigrants and practices of the abovementioned organisations, the requirements of the host society can be summarised as follows:

> "Learn the national language or dialect and then finish one of the local schools. Do that, regardless of age, gender, nationality, religion

etc. Further, do that regardless of one's qualifications previously obtained, one's preferences and abilities. Immigrants' own qualifications are not important, their ethnic resources and culture even less. They cannot contribute anything valuable to our society and culture, unless they assimilate and adapt to our needs on the market, where and how we want them."

In trying to follow these recommendations, one quickly meets major obstacles: gatekeepers, a policy of closed doors, one's own inabilities etc. Integration is then often perceived as impossible, senseless, time consuming and frustrating. This results in a feeling of relative deprivation (RUNCIMAN, 1966). If immigrants consequently do not move on, and many do, there is a growing possibility of exclusion and dependency on welfare or the family.

This criticism does not question the good intentions embodied in resolutions and legislation. Rather, it shows the contradictions within the ideological concept of ethnic social integration. It does not function as planned and is very costly. The meaning of local community within modern societies and especially in urban environments for social participation/integration is put in question (BLOCKLAND-POTTERS, 1998; HARVEY, 1997). The results call for new solutions, challenging the social quality of united Europe (BECK et al., 1997).

Immigrants' perspectives in employment, education and family security

Here I will present selected research results and cases gathered through interviews with immigrants in Denmark over the last three years. The position of refugees in camps, before they obtain permanent residence, is omitted at this point. One remark by a Bosnian refugee can nevertheless give a picture: "We have been, you know, in an 'integration'. That is something similar we used to have back there!" (referring to ideological integration in socialist Yugoslavia (HOLMEN, 1997)). It should be noted that "integration" has an ambiguous meaning —used in confining political dissidents during fascism, for example.

Employment and citizenship are two fundamental forms of status, around which most basic social and political rights revolve. Nevertheless, Nordic countries grant substantial social rights to the foreign permanent residents as well. One is given a work permit and basic health insurance, along with a tax number. The remaining political and more active social rights are postponed for at least three to five years (Probation Immigration Law, Denmark, 1993). Justification for that postponement has been expressed as follows: "Immigrants should understand the ideals and benefits of our society first. They should be happy to live here, since we offer them so many rights which they had no opportunity to experience before". Concerning their rights, immigrants will be informed "when we find it opportune" or "they may get a false idea and be misled by deceiving expectations. Immigrants can get a shock, they do not understand how it works here. We have to protect our society and them. Immigrants should not get used to asking too much, since they do not have experience of democratic communications." (REFUGEE COUNCIL, 1996; HOLMEN, 1997; SOCIAL CENTRE COPENHAGEN, 1998).

For this postponement and the first phase of immigrant settlement, a special analytical term, "purgatory", was coined. During this probation period (of three or five years), the foreigners are stigmatised, under suspicion and control. They are potentially "incriminated", since foreigners have to prove "their good intentions and behaviour" (not to commit any offence), remain in the country for eight months each year, not leave the common household, not divorce, learn the language, get qualifications, and possibly become or stay employed within their own professions.

In the first round, three responsible "mentors" are provided to the immigrant: the firm or school, if one obtains employment beforehand, the local government for asylum seekers or refugees, and the family in the case of reunification or ethnic marriage. The second phase depends upon the labour market and employers, family strength, educational selection (recognition of diplomas) and the eligibility of immigrants for further education. In most of these cases, the role of so-called "gatekeepers" is mentioned, who act within the policy of "closed doors" for foreign residents (REFUGEE COUNCIL, September 1998). These methods are often defined as tacit discrimination. They consist of the ways by which a non-native is discouraged from applying for different benefits or rights in the first place.

For example, youngsters from international high schools and those from third countries would hear at the International University office or at the opening days of Faculties the decisive evaluation: with "this" school, you have no chance to enter any faculty in Denmark! It is impossible for you to collect enough points to enter! Another illustration is when an immigrant calls for information concerning a job offer. M. comes from England, with a university degree which is not recognised. He speaks Danish very well, but the bank manager requires "perfect pronunciation and writing". When an accent in language is noticed or "the wrong name" given, the applicant is informed that the job is already taken. Often, unusually high language requirements are expected, difficult even for indigenous inhabitants. This last particularly affects Asian immigrants.

Employment

Unemployment rates among immigrants are high, increasing sharply in recent times. Within various segregated urban enclaves, these rates jumped from 30% to 70% in Sweden and Denmark during the late 1990s. Generally, these rates are twice those of the domestic population (BROOME et al., 1996; DENMARKS STATISTIK, December 1998). It is often stated that the latest migration flows consist of less qualified people than 15 years ago (YI, 1998). Despite this, those who are highly qualified, like many Iranian and Russian immigrants, also experience unemployment.

Yet there are more indirect effects of the "purgatory" probation period. Employers do not seriously consider a job candidate who has been in a country for less than three to five years. "Why don't you go back to your husband!" is a phrase delivered to the woman job seeker to discourage her and point to those responsible for her. On the other hand, when a person is wanted and needed, employers do not require language proficiency, recognition of diplomas and the like. Immigrants' social positions are therefore passive, the promised social rights difficult to realise. "It looks like a promised land, with deceiving hopes, though. Like walking on minefields" (HOLMEN, 1997).

Ten years ago, K. came from Russia with a Ph.D. in Russian literature, speaks Danish well (Danish Proficiency Test 1 and 2), is publishing, but cannot find a job. He is now 45 years old. An American architect with a Danish partner lost a job in an architect's office after a year and a half. The partnership came to an end, he worked as postal worker and speaks basic Danish. He could not open his own office since there were problems with recognition of his qualifications, and he did not have Danish Test 2. He was deported from Denmark since he was not married to a resident and was working outside his profession.

Research results in Sweden reveal the firm belief of employers that ethnic heterogeneity is "not productive". According to that belief, ethnic heterogeneity "disturbs the atmosphere and reduces efficiency". Since ethnic and cultural differences in the work environment are neither profit-making nor efficient, they are considered a legitimate reason for avoiding the employment of new residents. Less demanding temporary jobs in services are given instead to students, since they are often more qualified and do not depend on that position. It is also easier to discharge them (BROOME et al., 1996). In academic environments, after the first round of candidate selection for a position, the one with personal acquaintances is most likely to be taken. In post-bankrupt Sweden of the early 1990s, unemployment amongst immigrants rose sharply due mainly to the squeeze on public services. These services tend to be organised as private, non-profit firms which can survive if the staff are well organised, mobile, and good communicators —to persuade customers to make further service orders, while doing the work, for example.

> K. has a university degree from the UK, is 27 years old and of African origin. He married a Danish resident, works occasionally in a small private factory, on call. He speaks perfect English and is trying to learn Danish.

Foreigners can get employment only where there are no similar Danish applicants for that position. The employer has to negotiate a work permit for a foreigner with the Immigration Office. Language requirements are used as a convenient excuse not to employ foreigners even though the urban Scandinavian population is almost bilingual, with the second language being English. A representative of a Dutch, non-governmental anti-discrimination organisation expressed this view:

> "I would not worry so much about language requirements. It is a transitional reaction of closing up the system and defending own interests. With more common interests on the level of EU, there will be more co-operation. I would rather be concerned by the lack of social and political rights of ethnic groups. The absence of balanced debate in the public media is dangerous, allowing stigmatisations of ethnical issues" (Pisanu, 1997).

Mette is the experienced head of the Copenhagen Refugee Council and has gathered long-term trends on integration issues. When a highly qualified immigrant comes to her and wants a chance "to integrate", Mette's comments are very firm: "You are overqualified, over specialised. This environment will never accept you, neither will your Danish family." If one tries to volunteer, Mette thinks: "Maybe, but send your references first. If I get to employ you, I have to know what I receive from you. I have here a Polish engineer to change the electric bulbs around the house." Mette never answered the application which was send to her (REFUGEE COUNCIL, 1996).

Local employment centres are scattered around the city. When there, a foreign candidate fills out the form but almost no space is provided for education or qualifications obtained. The foreigner is interviewed about his physical condition with questions like: "Do you have any troubles with your back?" The signs in the windows offer mostly cleaning and unqualified jobs. For the newcomer, they still might not be available since "immigrants cannot understand written cleaning instructions".

The university-educated immigrant with a recognised diploma or Ph.D., years of experience and a decent knowledge of several languages might want to enrol in the Academic Syndicate, as advocated by many as a necessary precondition for further job seeking. There, one fills in a two-hour long questionnaire. After complex analysis, the immigrant is interviewed. A professional evaluation of his abilities is discussed, then finally comes the advice: "Why don't you learn the language first and then try to finish another school here!" There is neither an active programme for employment available nor any help from the Academic Syndicate in employment (MAGISTERFORENING COPENHAGEN, 1996).

Education

Scandinavian schools are in most cases only available to residents. There are some exchange programmes for students from EU countries and, exceptionally, some quotas for foreigners (in English teaching or private schools). All students have to be bilingual (Danish and English) since many textbooks are available only in English. To apply to university, new residents must have completed Danish Proficiency Test 1. On average, young immigrants take two or three years of hard study to pass that exam. After enrolment, students have the choice of writing and taking exams in English, while teaching is conducted in Danish.

> F. is a second year student from France and has a partner in Denmark. She cannot study at university without Danish, therefore she has to be employed. F. is following a Danish course, working, and studying via correspondence in France. After one year, she realises that her French diploma will not be accepted and that she would need to repeat a very similar programme in Denmark for another two years. She returns to France exhausted...

When a school receives an application from a new resident, years of education in the country of origin may be counted as an equivalent.

However, some diplomas from third countries may not be considered at all. Some 16 years of education and a university diploma are not enough for Denmark —the candidate is directed back to school for another two years and to Danish Test 1! Scandinavian countries have very long primary education, from nine to 10 years. In Denmark, high school is only three years. University is divided into three years for a Bachelor degree and two years for a graduate programme (Masters degree). Other EU countries may have eight years of elementary school, four years of high school and four years for a first university degree. Masters degrees take another two to three years.

> M. is an 24 year old engineer with a university diploma from the UK. His partner is Danish. M. is trying hard to learn Danish while working at Burger King. Two years of additional study are needed before he can have the same qualification recognised as that which he held on arrival in Denmark. In terms of time, M. needs four more years for that, due to language requirements. M. is desperate and his partner concludes that "he is not happy in Denmark". The Danish course finishes, M. returns to the UK. He has gained another language and a lot of prejudices.

In Denmark and Sweden, a Ph.D. can also be recognised outside university through an "internal evaluation of somebody's work" by a committee of three people who are not from university, nor have they themselves finished doctoral studies. Generally, an Anglo- American Ph.D. requires an additional four to six years of university study and may therefore be undervalued in comparison to Danish candidates. Discussion on these issues at the EU Commission cannot even start and there are many disputes.

It was only during 1999 that public debates, criticism and protests encouraged the Danish Ministry of Education to start considering how to evaluate qualifications from other countries. A qualification analysis of 8,950 representatives of the immigration population stated that 62 % had qualifications and, of those, 10 % had an academic education (BERLINGSKE TIDENDE, 8 January 1999, Kobenhavn).

Language

Scandinavian languages (particularly Danish) are very difficult to learn. Unreasonable standards of language proficiency therefore require many years of training. Danes are well aware of that (Danes may envy two things of others: warm weather and a beautiful language). Language schools are many, but with long waiting times of up to one year. There are limited possibilities of finding a suitable course: people of different ages, education, motivation and sometimes no common language are sitting together, while the teachers lack didactic support. "There is no system of phonetic notation that can do justice to spoken Danish... it is so unspeakably difficult, no foreigner can make it worse" (DYRBYE et al., 1997, p.63).

When language barriers are used as a convenient excuse for not giving new residents reasonable chances in employment and education, many of the human resources are lost: "Within the next decades, there will be a teaching period for everybody in the world. But if we are going to spend years learning each others' national languages, instead of using our knowledge and skills where and when they are needed", that will increase social costs and reduce our economic potential as well (PISANU, 1997).

Family

The family environment is difficult to capture in one pattern. The idea of family itself might be different between an ethnically mixed couple. Family reunification does not include children above the age of 18 (Denmark), or 16 (Sweden). Nordic people have high rates of divorce and remarriage, with a large proportion of single households. "Danish marriages lack the famous clutching power of the Lego brick. Marriage can be a necessary preliminary to divorce" (DYRBYE et al., 1997, p. 20; DENMARKS STATISTIK, 1998). Therefore, marriage represents a personal gamble or a social risk, rather than "a search for social security within our welfare states". "Foreigners only want to profit" is a typical stigma attributed to new residents from third countries. The probation period of three years leaves a foreign partner in complete submission vis-à-vis the resident partner, fostered by signing the "responsibility paper". During that time, a marriage can "be annulled" by legal authorities, if the foreign partner leaves home, even when obvious abuse is in question.

> Y. is 23 years old and comes from Africa. She used to work as a stewardess and was raised in a strong Catholic spirit. Her Dane noticed her in a family picture and found her, since he is a detective. "He walks around and listens to what other people say. At home, he uses to be tired, wants to be served and I have to entertain him." In Africa, he was passionate and said he cannot live without me, so I arrived in Denmark already pregnant. But here, he leaves me without

money, does not allow me to shop for any clothes, since "women should not get wrong ideas or bad habits", he says. "He threatens me constantly with divorce and deportation, calls me names like 'black ape'." Y. is terrified, abused, and suffers a spontaneous abortion. The hospital calls the social centre, but the staff cannot help her.

Hospitals, social centres or shelter homes report such cases to the Immigration Office and deportation is the result. Some shelter homes in Denmark apply quotas for abused persons of foreign origin. For six Danish battered women only one foreign abused person can be accepted. The social worker declares that "foreign residents are not even the subjects of our policies, we only help them to divorce and leave the country" (CHRISTIANSHAVN SOCIAL CENTRE, May 1999). At the Centre, the typical image of a Danish partner who seeks to marry a foreign partner is described: an elderly man with a history of several divorces, drinking or other problems —"they treat the foreign partner like shit", says the social worker in a resigned tone. The resident partner might threaten to annul his signed paper, which would annul the marriage. Even "romantic" marriages are in danger, where one partner has a hard time to keep personal integrity, promote equality in the relationship with the partner and before legal organisations.

Ethnically homogeneous families provide better emotional security and social networks. Inter-ethnic marriages are under legal surveillance due to the practice of "false" marriages. Dissidents were previously helped by Danes out of solidarity, but lately a real "marriage market" has emerged between East and West. The East "offers submission, obedience along with high qualifications", the West seeks "special sexual pleasure, money or three years of fun", as often defined in advertisements.

The question is whether state intervention to protect children and the foreign partner is in place, if it is needed and what is the responsibility of the indigenous partner. The shared responsibility for ethnic marriages was introduced in the early 1990s by a paper declaration at the Immigration Office in Denmark. By signing the paper, one declares personal responsibility for a partner and the Office determines whether the person signing has the appropriate financial means. The full meaning and consequences of this paper are not entirely revealed at this point, but it has provoked political and legal criticism from many sides. It might be discriminatory in at least two areas: certain constitutional rights (freedom of choosing a partner and family reunification) are in question for poor people and social rights (family support) for all taxpayers, are reduced.

Conclusions

Discrimination is very complicated and legally hard to prove. It might be forbidden by law, but it is seldom exactly defined. Different instances of so-called positive discrimination legislation are needed, as one solution proposes. There is an idea of active anti-ethnic discrimination policy in Copenhagen's Kommune (1998/99). It suggests, for example, that invitations in job advertisements for ethnic applicants be explicitly promoted.

I am hesitant about the explanation that Scandinavian countries are experiencing a revival of nationalism and that their inhabitants are becoming racists. Nor can recent multi-ethnic problems be revealed as the egoism of an ageing generation or the intolerance of a society of high collective consumption. Rather, I see the core of the problem in the asymmetry between economic determination of European societies within globalisation, which neglects social security and quality. People feel a loss of control over their lives and career prospects, there is increasing ambiguity concerning basic human values (BERRY, 1995). Mobility even within EU countries at present increases the split between family life and work prospects. The results are growing (female) unemployment, and falling family social security (TOWNSEND, 1997). It affects the possibilities of family formation itself, which strikes younger generations. Without a confirmed social policy, the EU cannot function economically in the long run.

As somebody put it nicely, after returning from many horrors of two wars: "There is no division between good and bad guys, there are circumstances where the same person can be both ways." Unemployment, economic stagnation, the forced and rising dominance of the global economy do not consider the human cost. The selective structure of the global economy and migratory flows are not complementary processes.

References

ANDERSSON, R. (1998): "Socio-spatial Dynamics: Ethnic Division of Mobility and Housing in post Palme Sweden". In: *Urban Studies*, 3, p. 397.
BECK, W.; MAESEN, L. VAN DER; WALKER, A. (1997): *The Social Quality of Europe*, Kluwer Law International, The Hague-London-Boston.
BERRY, R. (1995): *Economic Policies for Full Employment and the Welfare State*, London, PO Box 188, SW1A OSGA.
BLOCKLAND-POTTERS, T. (1998): "Social Innovation: Strategy to Prevent Social Exclusion?", paper for ISA Conference in Montreal, August.

BONACHICH, E.; LIGHT, I. (1988): *Immigrant Entrepreneurships: Koreans in Los Angeles 1965-1982*, California University Press, Berkeley, USA.
BROOME, P.; BÅCKLUND, A.-K.; LUNDH, C.; OHLSSON, R. (1996): *Varfor sitter brassen på bånken?* SNS Forlag, Stockholm.
CHRISTENSEN, B.V. (1997): "Population Mobility in Slovenije between 1974-1994". In: *Informativni bilten* 5-6, Ljubljana.
CLARK, W.A.V. (1998): "Mass Migration and Local Outcomes". In: *Urban Studies*, March.
DENMARK'S STATISTIK (1997): "Denmark levevilkår 1997", Jens Bonke; Danmarks Statistik Socialforskningsinstituttet: 271-287, Befolkning og valg 1997:14, 1998:18, København
DENMARK'S STATISTIK (December 1998): "Invandrere i Danmark", Marius Ejby Poulsen, Anita Lange, København.
DUNN, K.M. (1998): "Rethinking Ethnic Concentration: The case of Cabramatta, Sydney". In: *Urban Studies* 3, March.
DYRBYE, H.; HARRIS, S.; GOLZEN, T. (1977): *The Xenophobe's Guide to the Danes*, Ravette publishing, UK.
GARFINKEL, H. (1967): *Studies in Ethonomethodology*, Prentice-Hall, Engelwood Cliffs N.J.
HARVEY, D. (1997): "Contested Cities: Social Process and Spatial Form". In: *Transforming Cities*, ed. Nick Jewson and Susanne MacGregor. Routledge, London, New York.
HOLMEN, (1997): International Conference on Ethnic Women, Kobenhavn, Denmark.
KING, R. (1993): *Mass Migrations in Europe*, Belhaven Press, London.
KONTAKT nr.8, Internationalt magasin-november 1997; Trine Sick: Flugten til Europa, København, Københavns Kommune, Rådhuset, November 23., December 1.,1998; Handlingsplan for etnisk ligestilling, BR 7/99, J.nr.Ø342/98
LIGHT, I. (1979): *Ethnic Entrepreneurship in America*, UCLA University press, USA.
LIGHT, I. (1984): "Immigrant and Ethnic Enterprise in North America". In: *Ethnic and Racial Studies*, 7, pp.195-216.
MASTNAK, T. (1998): *Evropa med evolucijo in evtanazijo*, Studia Humanitatis-Apes, Ljubljana.
MEDVED, F. (1998): "Proposal for the Resolution on Immigration policy in Slovenija". In: *Poroèevalec* 38, Ljubljana.
PARK, R.E.; BURGESS, E.W.; MCKENZIE, R.D. (1925): *The City*, University of Chicago Press.
PISANU, F. (1997): "Equality and Discrimination in the Netherlands", paper on Ethnic Women conference, 7-10 November, Holmen, København, Denmark.
RUNCIMAN, W.G. (1966): *Relative Deprivation and Social Justice*, Routledge and Kegan Paul, London.
SOLDUE, 22 (June 1997): Magazine on and by multicultural women in Denmark: Documenting violence and battery of minority women, a document to the

Danish government in order to change the Immigration Law, art. 26, clauses 4, 5 and 6, concerning three years of a probationary regulation, against quotas for non-Danish women at shelter homes in Denmark, Copenhagen.

SAMFUNDSNØGLEN (1998): Statens Information, Nordisk Bogproduktion A/S, Haslev, Denmark.

TOWNSEND, A.R. (1997): *Making a Living in Europe*, Routledge, London/New York.

URBAN STUDIES (March 1998); vol.35, no.3, Special issue: International Migration and Ethnic Segregation: Impacts on Urban Areas.

VOGEL, J. (1991): "Living Conditions and Inequality in the Late 1980s", *Statistical Reports of the Nordic Countries*, no.55, Copenhagen.

YI, J.E. (1998): "Cosmopolitan Ethnicity, Cultural Politics, and The New (Global) Pluralism in American Urban Spaces", paper for ISA Conference in Montreal.

Public debates and individual cases published in the following newspapers: *Berlingske Tidende, Weekend avisen,* review *Magisterbladet, Aktuelt, Soldue, Kontakt* between 1996 and 1999.

Interviews with the representatives and staff in (cca 63) of some organisations (cca 6), immigrants at Language Schools and courses AOF-Amager, Danish Plus, KISS. More interviews were conducted at the Refugee Council, Social Centre Department, International University Office of Copenhagen, 1996-1999 and City Refugee Centre of Orebro, Sweden, 1994.

Diasporic identities and diasporic economies: the case of minority ethnic media

Charles Husband

Introduction

There is nothing new in recognising the central importance of the news media in multi-ethnic societies. In 1974 UNESCO published *Race As News*, which analytically and empirically outlined the central importance of the news media in shaping popular understandings of ethnic diversity. In particular it critically revealed the power of news media to provide a consensual view of the world which normalised the power and privilege of the dominant ethnic community, and made apparently reasonable the social exclusion of minority ethnic individuals. The role of the press in normalising the "natural" dominance of majority ethnic communities and in locating the status of minority ethnic communities as a problematic presence within national state systems was further elaborated in the 1977 UNESCO report, *Ethnicity and the Media*, and again in their 1986 report *Mass Media and the Minorities*. Beyond a more general analysis of eurocentrism within the media (SHOHAT/ STAM, 1994) there is now an understanding of the role and power of the news media in shaping popular understandings of ethnic diversity. The fact that this knowledge is generated from data drawn from around the world only serves to underline the depth of the insights available into this process (see for example DENNIS/PEASE, 1997; FRACHON/VARGAFTIG, 1993; FERGUSON, 1998; GANDY, 1998; JAKUBOWICZ et al., 1994; SANDLUND, 2000).

Historically, over the last three decades, much of the analysis of the operation and impact of the news media in multi-ethnic societies has focused upon the role of the "mainstream" media: namely the news media of the dominant ethnic community. This has of course been an important and necessary activity. But, to an extent, it has obscured both the existence and the importance of the minority ethnic media. As concern with the democratic role of the media in contemporary complex societies has focused upon their cultivation of an informed and active "public sphere" (KEANE, 1991; DAHLGREN/SPARKS, 1991), so there has been a need to recognise the diversity present within the media. The diverse ethnic demography of contemporary societies has constructed stable and multiple audiences defined by their shared language, ethnicity and experience of migration and settlement. And in many instances the existence of large minority ethnic communities has also made it necessary to recognise the extensive diversity *within* minority ethnic communities. This is a diversity shaped by, amongst other things, generation, gender, class and religious identities. These internal distinctions not only represent the reality of minority ethnic identity politics, they also form the demographic basis for commercially viable audiences. This is a demographic basis for the emergence and survival of minority ethnic media aimed at distinctive target audiences. Thus it is appropriate that in recent years there has been an increasing recognition of the critical importance of the role of minority ethnic media within multi-ethnic societies (HUSBAND, 1996; European Monitoring Centre on Racism and Xenophobia/WDR, 1999). This paper starts from an acceptance of this reality and will explore both the current situation in the United Kingdom, and the general principles that might be developed to guide our understanding of the current, and potential, roles of the minority ethnic news media.

The multicultural context

The fact that all Western European countries are *de facto* multi-ethnic societies in no way means that there is a consensus about the appropriate political mechanisms for managing ethnic diversity. Whilst the European Union may have developed a language, and an incipient policy, around issues of social exclusion, at the national level multiculturalism continues to have different meanings and draws upon different values in each member state (HECKMANN/BOSSWICK, 1995; WRENCH/SOLOMOS, 1993). The ease with which the British from the early 1960s developed a "race relations industry" and happily spoke of "race relations", and by the 1980s were invoking the relevance of "a black perspective", was not echoed in France with its republican tradition of *laïcité*. And nor was ethnic diversity easily convertible into an inclusive multicultural citizenship in a Germany based upon a conception of the national *Volk*. From a different perspective it might also be argued that countries like Britain and the Netherlands, with a history of empire and colonialism, were sensitive to accusations of racism, whilst countries with a history of being dominated, like Norway and Ireland, could imagine themselves to be historically inoculated against being nasty to minorities. In essence the last four decades show that the majority ethnic populations, in coming to terms with the growing ethnic diversity of their country, have drawn on their distinctive histories and dominant values in developing their own route toward multicultural policies.

This specificity of each national response to the emergence of contemporary multiculturalism is paralleled by the distinctive history, and current demography, of the minority ethnic communities in these same countries. The collective nouns "immigrant" and "ethnic minority" dangerously invite an assumption of shared identities and histories among those caught in these labels. The reality is, however, very different. The history of the construction of minority ethnic populations contains the roots of significant differences in self definition, and even legal standing. Indigenous peoples, whether the Australian Aborigines, Native Americans, or Sami in the Nordic States, have a strong sense of their very distinctive identity and relation to the state. Indeed, they often have a specific legal standing in relation to the state. National minorities within the state may have resulted from federation or conquest. They are typically citizens of the state but may feel more or less ambiguous about their relation to it. As devolution in the United Kingdom is revealing, a long established federation of "nations" can leave intact very strong independent national identities, something all too evident in Spain and Belgium. And in post-war Europe migration of "immigrants" has very significantly changed the ethnic profile of European states. But migration for work from ex-colonies and near neighbours differs dramatically from the more recent transcontinental migration of refugees.

All these different histories shape the local, and global, territorial connectedness of specific communities. These histories are coded into the distinct identities of each ethnic community and they contribute to the shaping of boundaries with others, and to the internal differentiation within the community. In the contemporary literature of ethnicity the ideas of hybridity and diaspora have been central to the discussion of identities (WERBNER/MODOOD, 1997). The concept of hybridity demands that in any discussion of ethnicity the interaction of multiple facets of identity are recognised and acknowledged. For the media this is a pointer to the existence of multiple audiences *within* ethnic communities, defined by combinations of, *inter alia*, gender, generation, class, religious commitment and sexual preference. And the concept of diaspora acts as a persistent reminder that each of these hybrid persons is located within a particular sense of time and space. In an increasingly global world it is important to recognise the affiliation to others like oneself who live in distant locations. The connectedness of people over time and space provides unique diasporic linkages which inform individuals' media needs and media consumption (MORLEY/ROBINS, 1995). As will become apparent below, the reality of the hybrid and diasporic formation of ethnic identities is recognised by the new media, and is echoed and reaffirmed in the distinct target audiences of the minority ethnic media. And, as we shall see below, this diasporic connectedness is also reflected in the political economy of minority ethnic media as transcontinental corporate links facilitate the production, and economic viability, of minority ethnic newspapers.

However, before proceeding any further with this argument it is important to pause and problematise the use of the concept of diaspora. It is an idea, and a discourse, of dispersed identities that is both "loose in the world" (CLIFFORD, 1994, p. 306) and all too easily loosely employed. CUNNINGHAM/SINCLAIR (2000) in their recent text have provided a most valuable cautionary analysis of the definition and use of the concept of diaspora in a section they entitle *Delineating Diaspora*. I will draw selectively on that review to clarify the conceptual framework I wish to employ here. In moving toward a definition of diaspora Cunningham and Sinclair provide some valuable criteria: notably they argue that:

> Certainly, some sense of difference, marginality and displaced belonging is essential to the concept, including a strong identification with a homeland and the corresponding resistance of diasporic groups to complete assimilation by the host nation. However, the most literal element in any definition must be that of dispersal (CUNNINGHAM/ SINCLAIR, 2000, p. 10).

And later they note a

> sense of cultural adaptiveness, innovation and hybridity [which], along with the notions of dispersal and unassimilated difference, is at the heart of the concept of diaspora, ... (ibid., p. 16).

This emphasis upon a dynamic sense of cultural adaptiveness and continually creative hybridity as characteristic of the nature of the diasporic process is underlined by their explicit warning of the essentialising conceptions of culture that can be seen to be deployed by some of those examining the experience of diaspora. There is a clear danger of invoking some notion of an historically continuous cultural core as the binding *essence* that has contained a diasporic identity across time and territory. The cultural identity of diasporic communities must be seen as a part of the diasporic process rather than as a *property* of diasporic people.

Particularly when the diversity *within* diasporic communities is recognised and articulated through the language of hybridity, the dynamic nature of cultural processes within diasporic communities is more readily revealed. For example, whilst there may be a popular association of diaspora with global movements of a predominately proletarian nature, it is important to remember, among other things, the class variation *within* and *between* diasporic communities. The settled minority ethnic populations of people with Pakistani and Iranian heritage in Britain are but one example of migrations with very different histories and different class profiles.

Indeed, throughout Cunningham and Sinclair's text there is continuing evidence of the need to explicitly *historise* the distinctive nature of specific diasporas. A post-modern celebration of the diasporic *zeitgeist* is no substitute for a careful and detailed analysis of specific diasporic trajectories and current realities. RAY (2000) provides just such specificity in his analysis of the media practice of Fiji Indian communities in Australia. He argues that:

> ... the different postcolonial diasporas are not "splinters" in a transnational world, ready to rearticulate their identity on the lines of extra-territority or nomadism; on the contrary it is the historical subjectivity of a diaspora which holds the key to its cultural life [...] Hence the alienation that postcolonial people face in the multicultural West is multilayered; citings of the more visible signs of racism do not register its historical depth (RAY, 2000, p. 141).

Analyses such as Ray's stand as powerful warnings against any easy summation of diasporic experiences; and in his case particularly against assuming any common "Indian" diaspora.

In a final selective extrapolation from Cunningham and Sinclair it is relevant for the argument I wish to develop to note their observations on the dual relationship of diaspora to global capital. We are familiar with the very many instances where international flows of people have been a consequence of global investment patterns and international inequalities. From slavery, through indentured labour to contemporary patterns of Indian labour in the Middle East, or the selective recruitment of Asian skilled labour into Australia, there is ample evidence of diasporic movement as an *effect* of capital and global market forces. However, Cunningham and Sinclair usefully remind us that diasporic movement is also a *cause* of the globalisation of capital. Quoting KOTKIN (1992, p. 17) they note that:

> The continuous interaction of capitalism with dispersed ethnic groups —not just the staid history of financial flows or the heroic stories of nation builders— constitutes one of the critical elements in the evolution of the global economy (CUNNINGHAM/SINCLAIR, 2000, p. 12).

Thus, the inter-regional connections that are found within diasporic communities may be networks of commerce as well as networks of culture and kinship (cf. APPADURAI, 1996).

Consequently, in developing a conceptual framework for generating insights into the relation of diasporic identities and diasporic economies, the conception of diaspora invoked needs to be capable of reflecting the dynamics briefly reviewed here. Diasporic communities are not merely geographically dispersed fragments of a common core culture. The internal fragmentation of generation, gender and class need to be recognised as dynamic engines of social mobilisation and key sites of identity negotiation. Hybridity is not only a feature of *members* of a diasporic community, it is characteristic of the "community" *per se*. Essentialising invocations of core cultures are contrary to a fully historised understanding of the diasporic experience. And finally, the political economy of diasporic media environments cannot be seen as an external commercial nexus that responds to the prior existence of diasporic communities. The political economy of these media is also an element of the diasporic process itself: the "community" working through capital, as well as capital adapting to diasporic communities.

In an ambiguous juxtaposition to their argument in relation to the specific historisity of diasporic communities (CUNNINGHAM/SINCLAIR, 2000). SINCLAIR et al. (1996) have also argued for the effective existence of geolinguistic regions for media which are operative in a zone between the local and the global. Interestingly, they argue that:

> ... it is cultural similarities in general, not just language in particular, that bind geolinguistic regions into television markets (SINCLAIR et al., 1996, p. 13).

That language should provide a significant barrier to the potential size of any media product's audience is reasonable, if not exactly self-evident. Particularly in the print media, literacy in the language of production is a *sine qua non* of consumption. Thus, major world languages such as Arabic, Chinese, French, Hindi, English and Spanish enjoy a market advantage not shared by, for example, Norwegian, Sami or Nepalese.

However, Sinclair *et al.* are additionally arguing that there are ranges of "cultural proximity" that bound potential media audiences, such as Pan-Sino Chinese audiences, a Latin American regional space and an American/European/Australian region. An inherent dynamic in such geolinguistic regions is the existence of a degree of commonality in the audience's "reading" of media products. Thus, it is not an argument about high levels of cultural commonality across these regions; but rather the existence of thinner layers of aesthetic and historical resonances.

An additional element in the configuring of such regions is the role of regional entrepreneurs and "the restratification of audiences into 'imagined communities' beyond national boundaries" (*ibid.*, p. 24). One feature of the operation of such entrepreneurs is their capacity to demonstrate the inadequacy of any simplistic thesis of *cultural imperialism* which sees media flows emanating from the affluent "North" and dominating the poor "South". Bollywood and the extra-continental reach of the tele-novella are just two of the more obvious instances of powerful media flows that demonstrate other sites of global transmission. Major corporate players, and local diasporic broadcasters and distributors, are key elements in the construction of the media infrastructures that feed the geolinguistic regions outlined by Sinclair *et al*.

Thus, in any state the majority and minority ethnic communities come together within a unique environment shaped by the historical construction of the state and a unique route to becoming ethnically diverse. Consequently the language and values that shape the multicultural policy in each state are a particular expression of that history. There are now innumerable injunctions and formal instruments emanating from the Council of Europe and the European Union which point to the central role of the news media in such multi-ethnic societies (e.g. EUROPEAN MONITORING CENTRE ON RACISM AND XENOPHOBIA, 1999). And the cumulative message of the analysis of the operation of the *majority* ethnic news media is that they are not to be relied upon to meet the informational and socio-political needs of minority ethnic communities. Thus if the aspirations for the functioning of the news media in multi-ethnic societies, expressed in these policy statements, are to be met, there must be a viable and vital minority ethnic media.

The informational and cultural needs of minority ethnic communities

Given what has been said above about the great diversity within minority ethnic communities, it is hardly likely that their expectations of the news media can be reduced to a single inclusive statement. However, given the history of migration and the current diasporic identity of many minority ethnic communities, it is possible to sketch an initial outline model. In fact a transcontinental comparative analysis of the informational needs of refugees carried out by UNESCO (HUSBAND, 1988) provides a useful starting point. Given their experience of disruption and dislocation, refugees have quite specific immediate informational needs; these include:

—Information relating to such immediate daily needs as food, health, living quarters and clothing.
—Information relating to the local reception and treatment of refugees.
—General information on the receiving country's social and political situation.

However, the analysis of the studies from different continents clearly indicated that many refugees become long-term migrants, and settlers in their countries of refuge. In this respect they come to share many of the characteristics of other diasporic minority ethnic communities. Their initial reason for migration may have been radically different, but they come to share many of the experiences of marginality and social exclusion in their country of settlement. Consequently the findings of the UNESCO study have more general applicability.

That report distinguished between the mid and long term provision of information about the receiving country, and information about the *country of emigration*. Clearly in relation to information about the receiving country there is a need for information about the values, structures and politics of that society. This would include: information about social and cultural issues, politics, the legal and juridical process, the economy and labour market, the educational system and the health system. Any systematic scrutiny of the minority ethnic news media in Britain would reveal that these functions are being served for both recently established and long settled minority communities. From a partisan identification with their readers the minority ethnic press provide both information about, and a critique of these facets of British life.

For both refugees and migrants their diasporic identities sustain for many an on-going need for information about their country of emigration. The UNESCO report noted *inter alia*:

—Information about their country of origin is of continuing value to refugee populations, and is therefore a long term requirement.
—In many instances the indigenous press and broadcast media of the country of origin are highly relevant to, and valued by, refugees.
—For many sending societies their refugees are a problematical population of economic, political or religious exiles, and hence information directed to them will be partial and controlled.

In the context of world flows of refugee populations these comments from a 1988 review have enduring relevance. Equally, as CASTLES (2000) has demonstrated, the processes of labour migration have also generated very diverse patterns of multi-ethnic demographies in nation states around the world. As has already been noted above, the unique circumstances of these migratory processes, and the social and political repertoire of receiving countries, have generated uneven patterns of inclusion and exclusion of these settled minority ethnic populations. Several decades after initial migration, minority ethnic communities continue to experience themselves as objects of political intolerance and marginalisation (see e.g. BLOMMAERT/VERSCHUEREN, 1998; HARGREAVES, 1995; HAGE, 1998). Not surprisingly, therefore, members of such communities have a real sense of their diasporic location, simultaneously within and outside their country of residence, and often of citizenship. Whilst human geographers stress the "spatiality" underpinning such existential dynamics (JACKSON/PENROSE, 1993), the fragmenting of shared experience by interactions of gender and generation provides a rich tapestry of adaptive responses to being "diasporic". In relation to media consumption these distinctive dynamics are apparent in the patterning of selective exposure to specific media and the needs they fulfil.

In the British context it is apparent that both migrant minorities and refugees continue to have enduring interests in their country of origin (GILLESPIE, 2000; STREBERNY, 2000). For many who migrated to Britain in the 1960s and 70s, and for their children, the remittance of money to relatives "at home" remains a concrete link to their country of origin. And as will be seen below, information from and about that country remains a powerful determinant of the newspaper choice of first generation migrants. Additionally for them, and subsequent generations, a diasporic interest in, and participation in, the political process of their country of initial origin may be a matter of concern that is reflected in their choice of newspaper and broadcast media. Certainly for both refugees and migrants there is within the minority ethnic media an explicit awareness of the relevance, and demand for, information from both the country of origin, and from diasporic communities elsewhere in the world. Britain is of course also a platform from which migrants and refugees generate information for transmission back into their "homeland"; the licensing of Medtv in London being a classic instance of this process.

In particular, the informational and cultural needs of minority ethnic consumers of newscopy in Britain reflect the hybridity and diasporic connectedness that defines each community. Language and culture are powerful variables in shaping their selective use of the media; but so too is the specific historical process that has shaped their current identities within Britain. The extensive diversity of minority ethnic news media in Britain is a reflection both of the audiences' communication needs, and of their viability as distinct target audiences.

Minority ethnic news media in Britain: ethnic hybridity and audience fragmentation

Within Britain there is a very considerable infrastructure of minority ethnic media. If we are to believe *The Media Guide 2000* there are 115 newspapers designated "Ethnic Press", 16 ethnic radio stations and 6 ethnic television stations. This is almost certainly an underestimate. If we complement this listing with the index of minority ethnic media produced by the Commission for Racial Equality we find that it lists *newspapers* and *periodicals* by language group. This listing generates the following table:

Table 1. Ethnic media by language

Arabic	2 dailies 2 weeklies 1 fortnightly	Greek Gujarati	2 weeklies 1 daily 2 weeklies	Punjabi	3 weeklies 1 fortnightly 2 monthlies
Bengali	2 dailies 5 weeklies	Hindi	1 fortnightly 2 weeklies	Turkish	1 daily 1 weekly
Chinese	1 daily 1 bi-monthly 1 monthly	Italian	1 weekly	Urdu	1 daily 2 weeklies 1 monthly

*English (to specific audiences)

African	Asian	Black/Afro-Caribbean	Irish	Jewish	Other
1 fortnightly 1 monthly	2 dailies 6 weeklies 2 fortnightlies 7 monthlies 1 bi-monthly 3 quarterlies	4 weeklies 1 monthly 4 quarterlies	3 weeklies 1 fortnightly	3 weeklies	1 weekly 3 monthlies 3 bi-monthlies 2 quarterlies

* This is an incomplete coding, but is indicative of the range.

Thus even this approximate survey offers a picture of the very considerable diversity of the minority ethnic newspaper and periodical operation in Britain. And this does not include all the *national* press of the diasporically connected nations that may be found in small numbers in newsagents in specific minority community neighbourhoods; or those that are taken by subscription. This rich repertoire of newspapers is an indication that the internal hybridity found within minority ethnic communities is to some extent reflected in the diversity of print media available to serve them.

Whilst the existential diversity present *within* minority ethnic communities may present a challenge to mainstream media in their efforts to "be sensitive to minority ethnic interests", it also provides fragmented niche audiences that may be targeted and served. The demography of each community sets limits on the commercial viability of these niche markets as age, gender and class intersect in fracturing the assumed "ethnic community". Transnational economics are one solution to this challenge.

There are clearly papers that in their editorial position and identified target audience seek to address the informational needs of first generation migrants and older members of minority ethnic communities. For example *The (Weekly) Gleaner*, the *Daily Jang* and the daily *Sing Tao* address the concerns of just such a segment of the African-Caribbean, the Pakistani and the Chinese communities respectively. In meeting this need it may not be irrelevant that they are all affiliated papers of their parent papers in the "sending country". Though legally separate corporate entities they all benefit from a close liaison with the news production of the parent paper; drawing on their "home" additions as a source of copy. Although this activity is costed as a transaction between independent corporate entities there are clearly great economies of scale to be derived from such a linkage.

These papers have developed with their readers; being established in 1951 (*The Gleaner*), 1971 (the *Daily Jang*) and 1975 (*Sing Tao*). For both the *Jang* and *Sing Tao* the linguistic competence of succeeding generations in the community language constitutes a challenge to their extending their readership beyond their long established readers. In response to this the *Jang* now produces a number of pages each day in English in order to widen its potential audience. This is a strategy that has been paralleled by *Parikiaki*, a newspaper serving the Greek-Cypriot and Greek communities in Britain. By publishing in two languages it is possible not only to extend the readership but also to open up the possibility of shaping the content to the readers of each section. More "home country" news in the community language, and more British related content in the English section.

This issue of age and generation is clearly a major variable in the ways in which newspapers position themselves in relation to their ethnically defined audience. This convergence of consumer need and marketing rationale is very clearly indicated, for example, in the operation of the Ethnic Media Group. This newspaper group owns the *Asian Times* and the *Caribbean Times*, both papers aimed at readerships of somewhere over thirty five years old with a good deal of international news to complement the news from Britain. These are papers for a maturer diasporic consciousness, offering information from the "sending society" and the wider diaspora. As a quite deliberate complement to these two titles the Ethnic Media Group also owns the *Eastern Eye* and *New Nation*, aimed respectively at the younger, British focused, members of the Asian and African Caribbean communities. The editorial strategy of the newsgroup eloquently illustrates the different audiences that are commercially identifiable *within* minority ethnic communities. And, as in the case of the earlier examples above, there are clearly benefits of economy of production and synergy in both news gathering and marketing.

Whilst there are instances of small newspapers being produced by dedicated individuals with family and friends (*Ravi* in Bradford being a good example), the British minority ethnic media environment is also characterised by a great deal of economic and managerial corporate acumen. Cross fertilisation between the minority ethnic press in Britain and media enterprises in the "sending country" are easy to find. Radio, television and other media interests are interwoven in transactional liaisons that provide a significant part of the fabric of the British minority ethnic press. Diasporic identities are in many instances benefiting from the transnational corporate arrangements that in the globalised world represent an economic expression of the dispersal of peoples over the globe. Recent interviews with professionals in this newsmedia sector provide clear indications of the importance of this transnational political economy for both current and future press activity. Indeed the advent of information technology is already causing some to anticipate a future radical repositioning of print as some monthly and weekly imprints may move over to new technologies; where the savings on paper and print hold out the possibility of new economies of production.

In reflecting on interviews with journalists and managers in this section it is apparent that a further significant cleavage in editorial stance and market profile may be suggested. Some of this press is unequivocally and unashamedly partisan, seeing itself as "the voice of the community". In taking this position they are acknowledging the distinct processes of social exclusion that define the situation of "their community" in relation to the majority population. They are also indicating, sometimes vehemently, the failure of the majority "mainstream" press to accurately and appropriately reflect this reality. For some other major players such political positioning, *campaigning journalism*, is passé and not relevant to the interests of their younger readers, who they define as British and young as well as having minority ethnic identity. This divergence is apparent in the house style of particular papers and its implications for the future development of this sector are not necessarily easy to read.

In positioning themselves within the news media of specific minority ethnic communities, it is clear that religious affiliation and party politics are both significant mechanisms for defining a particular paper's target audience. For example, within the "Asian" press there are papers that claim a secular identity and others serving the same community that have an avowedly religious stance. Equally the party politics of the "sending country" are not irrelevant to the internal dynamics of settled minority ethnic communities in Britain. Here again differing party political positions are expressed through different papers; and indeed some of these papers have formal links to the political parties in their "sending country". The globalised nature of contemporary identities, and the specific territorial connections of diasporic communities, can be seen to be reflected in the rich flora of the British minority ethnic press. There is very often real choice to be had amongst papers offering a choice of language, a choice of territorial focus, and a choice of editorial commitment to religion and politics.

Conclusion

We have in the introduction noted the "cultural adaptiveness and continually creative hybridity" that is characteristic of the diasporic experience, and minority ethnic news media are an intrinsic element of this dynamic. Generational differences in perspective may be inserted into the consciousness of younger generations in ways that have little meaning for those who initially migrated. Religious and ethnic zealotry may be imported and exported. And transnational imagery linkages may be made with "the excluded" of other countries with whom there is a social contact. The news media are a creative tool of the identity politics of diasporic communities and their use and impact is reflective of the hybridity within them.

It is possible to draw from this British case study some generalisable implications. Changing technologies and the globalised political economy of the media are providing an institutional infrastructure that can respond to the dynamic complexity of contemporary ethnic identities. As the politics of difference is developed and articulated uniquely within the distinctive cultural and political environment of nation states, so too media environments are being transformed at different rates. Racism and xenophobia remain visible and potent forces in these states and the active monitoring of the role of the media in promoting and challenging racism remains a necessary continuing task. However, seeking to expunge racism does not necessarily lead to an explicit view of how diversity should be managed. As I have argued elsewhere (HUSBAND, 1998), discussions of the role of the media in multi-ethnic societies are strongly shaped by assertive claims of the right to speak, and to control the representation of oneself and one's community. There is a necessary centripetal, inward-looking dynamic to this argument that is unfortunately not matched by an equivalent commitment to seek to understand the other. I have argued that a multi-ethnic public sphere requires *both* the opportunity for a diversity of voices in the media, *and* a shared disposition to seek to comprehend the experience of others. The alternative is that ethnic hybridity and progressive audience fragmentation will generate a tower of Babel of self-serving parallel and isolated public spheres. A rich diversity of media does not of itself guarantee mutual comprehension. In recognising the interaction of hybrid identities and increasing audience fragmentation, two complementary principles for a viable media environment in a multi-ethnic society are suggested:

—Autonomous minority ethnic media that are capable of enabling a dialogue *within* ethnic communities, and of reflecting the internal diversity to be found there.
—Complementary media which actively aim to promote dialogue *across* ethnic boundaries.

Such a media environment can only function equitably in a society that has an understanding of the politics of difference, and which has transcended naive universalist assumptions about the nature of equity in multi-ethnic societies.

References

APPADURAI, A. (1996): *Modernity at Large.* University of Minnesota Press, Minneapolis.
BLOMMAERT, J.; VERSCHUEREN, J. (1998): *Debating Diversity: Analysing the Discourse of Tolerance.* Routledge, London.
CASTLES, S. (2000): *Ethnicity and Globalisation.* Sage, London.
CLIFFORD, J. (1994): "Diasporas", *Cultural Anthropology,* 9(3), pp. 302-338
COTTLE, S. (2000): *Ethnic Minorities and the Media.* Open University Press, Buckingham.
CUNNINGHAM, S.; SINCLAIR, J. (2000): *Floating Lives: the Media and Asian Diasporas.* University of Queensland Press, St. Lucia, Queensland.
DAHLGREN, P.; SPARKS, C. (eds.) (1991): *Communication and Citizenship: Journalism and the Public Sphere in the New Media Age.* Routledge, London.
DENNIS, E.; PEASE, E.C. (1997): *The Media in Black and White.* Transaction Books, New Brunswick.
EUROPEAN MONITORING CENTRE ON RACISM AND XENOPHOBIA (1999): *Cultural Diversity Against Racism.* Westdeutscher Rundfunk, Köln.
FERGUSON, R. (1998): *Representing "Race".* Arnold, London.
FRACHON, C.; VARGAFTIG, M. (1993): *Télévision d'Europe et Immigration.* INA/ Association Dialogue entre les Cultures, Paris.
GANDY, O.H. (1998): *Communication and Race.* Arnold, London.
GILLESPIE, M. (2000): "Transnational communications and diaspora communities". In: *Ethnic Minorities and the Media,* ed. S. Cottle. Open University Press, Buckingham.
HAGE, G. (1998): *White Nation.* Pluto Press, Annandale NSW.
HARGREAVES, A.G. (1995): *Immigration, "Race", and Ethnicity in Contemporary France.* Routledge, London.
HECKMANN, F.; BOSSWICK, W. (1995): *Migration Policies: a Comparative Perspective.* Ferdinand Enke Verlag, Stuttgart.
HUSBAND, C. (1988): "The media and refugees: communication and human rights in the refugee's world". In: *Information, Communication and the Human Rights of Migrants,* ed. T. Hujanen. Bureau Lausannois pour les Immigrés/ UNESCO, Lausanne, p. 153-190.
HUSBAND, C. (1996): *A Richer Vision.* John Libbey/UNESCO, London.
HUSBAND, C. (1998): "Differentiated citizenship and the multi-ethnic public sphere". In: *The Journal of International Communication* 5(1/2), pp. 134-148.
JACKSON, P.; PENROSE, J. (1993): *Constructions of Race, Place and Nation.* UCL Press, London.

JAKUBOWICZ, A. et al. (1994): *Racism, Ethnicity and The Media.* Allen and Unwin, Sydney.
KEANE, J. (1991): *The Media and Democracy.* Polity Press, Cambridge.
KOTKIN, J. (1992): *Tribes: How Race, Religion and Identity Determine Success in the New Global Economy.* Random House, New York.
MORLEY, D.; ROBINS, K. (1995): *Spaces of Identity: Global Media, Electronic Landscapes and Cultural Boundaries.* Routledge, London.
RAY, M. (2000): "Bollywood down under: Fiji Indian cultural history and popular assertion". In: *Floating Lives: the Media and Asian Diasporas*, ed. S. Cunningham and J. Sinclair. University of Queensland Press, St. Lucia, Queensland.
SANDLUND, T. (2000): *Racism och etnicitet; den finlandssvenska tidningspressen.* CEREN, Helsingfors Universitet, Helsingfors.
SHOHAT, E.; STAM, R. (1994): *Unthinking Eurocentrism.* Routledge, London.
SINCLAIR, J.; JACKA, E.; CUNNINGHAM, S. (1996): *New Patterns in Global Television: Peripheral Vision.* Oxford University Press, Oxford.
STREBERNY, A. (2000): "Media and diasporic consciousness: an exploration among Iranians in London". In: *Ethnic Minorities and the Media*, ed. S. Cottle. Open University Press, Buckingham.
UNESCO (1974): *Race As News.* Paris.
UNESCO (1977): *Ethnicity and the Media.* Paris.
UNESCO (1986): *Mass Media and the Minorities.* Bangkok.
WERBNER, P.; MODOOD, T. (1997): *Debating Cultural Hybridity.* Zed Books, London.
WRENCH, J.; SOLOMOS, J. (1993): *Racism and Migration in Western Europe.* Berg, Oxford.

Commodity culture and South Asian transnationality

Peter Jackson

Introduction

This chapter aims to bring together two recent strands of work concerning commodity culture and transnationality to provide some fresh insights into the nature of contemporary multiculturalism and diversity in the city. Since Marx's seminal work in Volume 1 of *Capital* (1867) it has become commonplace to juxtapose the apparently trivial, everyday nature of the commodity form with its fundamental centrality to capitalist forms of exchange. Paraphrasing Marx, Don Slater outlines how the process of commodification lies at the heart of contemporary capitalism:

> Commodified labour produces commodities, things that are produced for sale and therefore for consumption by someone other than the person whose labour produced it. Instead of being organically and transparently linked within praxis, the relation between production and consumption is indirect and mediated through markets, money, prices, competition and profit —the whole apparatus of commodity exchange (1997, p. 107).

Recent years have seen an expansion of the reach of the commodity form into more and more areas of life —including health, the arts and education— that were previously thought to be "beyond commodification". This now includes the commodification of various forms of social and cultural difference, associated with gender, sexuality and ethnicity, as revealed by even the most cursory exploration of the contemporary advertising (JACKSON/TAYLOR, 1996). It is these wider connections between culture and economy that are being addressed by references to "consumer culture" (LURY, 1996) or by attempts to map the economies, practices and spaces of contemporary commodity cultures (JACKSON, 1999).

One of the defining characteristics of contemporary commodity culture is its increasing transnationality. "Transnationalism" is a vogue word that, in its current form at least, entered the social sciences in the 1990s. Previously restricted to the operation of transnational corporations, other forms of transnationality have since been identified such that the word is now applied to a wide range of interactions (economic, political, social, cultural) that link people or institutions across the borders of nation-states (VERTOVEC, 1999). While some authors have sought to restrict the term to the regular cross-border activities and institution building of particular groups of transnational migrants, such as Mexican-Americans in southern California or Haitian and Dominican migrants in New York (PORTES et al., 1999), others have sought to extend the term to a encompass a wider "social field" (BASCH et al., 1994). So, for example, Roger ROUSE describes the forces shaping Mexican-Americans' lives as "coming to affect everyone who inhabits the terrain encompassed by Mexico and the United States" (1991, p. 8). He continues:

> The comfortable modern imagery of nation-states and national languages, of coherent communities and consistent subjectivities, of dominant centers and distant margins no longer seems adequate... During the last twenty years, we have all moved irrevocably into a new kind of social space (p. 18, emphasis added).

The identification of a transnational social field occupied by a variety of participants, only some of whom would define themselves as ethnically-identified transnational migrants, is strikingly similar to Avtar BRAH's notion of "diaspora space" which, she argues, is "inhabited" not only by diasporic subjects (or so-called "ethnic minorities") but also by those who are constructed and represented as "indigenous" (1996, p. 16).

Recognition of the growing role of transnationality in shaping social and cultural identities as well as economic relations across national borders should not be taken as evidence of the declining significance of the nation-state. For, as Nina GLICK-SCHILLER et al. have argued: "While borders may be cultural constructions, they are constructions that are backed by force of law, economic and political power, and regulating and regularizing institutions" (1997, p. 159) —many of which are still fundamentally shaped by nation governments. Transnational practices such as those explored in this chapter are embedded in enduring asymmetries of power —forces that are still closely articulated with state formations and national boundaries (SMITH/ GUARNIZO, 1998). In particular, transnational identities and practices are, as Linda

BASCH et al. (1994) have shown, configured by hegemonic categories of race and ethnicity that are deeply embedded in the nation-building process of both "sending" and "receiving" countries. Approaching transnationality through the lens of commodity culture lends force to the argument about the need to identify a wider transnational social field without losing sight of the asymmetries of power that continue to shape the nature and content of social relations within those fields. For, as GLICK-SCHILLER et al. have argued:

> The constant and various flows of ... goods and activities have embedded within them relationships between people. These social relations take on meaning within the flow and fabric of daily life, as linkages between different societies are maintained, renewed, and reconstituted in the context of families, of institutions, of economic investments, business, and finance and of political organisations and structures including nation-states (1992, p. 11).

Without such "grounding" in the realities of everyday life and the structural reconfigurations that characterise contemporary capitalism, the concept of transnationalism becomes too abstracted and dematerialized, leading to the kind of watered-down social science that ONG and NONINI refer to disparagingly as "lite anthropology" (1997, p. 13) and which Katharyne MITCHELL refers to the "hype of hybridity" (1997). Combining recent work on transnationalism and commodity culture, however, leads to some novel insights into our present concern with multiculturalism and "diversity in the city".

Difference and diversity

The remainder of this chapter falls into two parts: a theoretical argument about the nature of transnational commodity culture, and an empirical section based on current research into the transnationalities involved in British-Asian commodity culture, focusing on the food and fashion sectors. I want to begin, though, by trying to establish a contrast between the concepts of diversity and difference. Drawing in particular on the work of BRAH (1992), I want to suggest that the term "diversity" is a problematic one, associated with liberal notions of multiculturalism that fail to deal adequately with the unequal social relations of power within which questions of cultural difference are invariably embedded. For, as James Donald and Ali Rattansi argue in the introduction to their book on *"Race", culture and difference*: "a multicultural celebration of diversity ... fail[s] to address the continuing hierarchies of power and legitimacy that still exist among ... different centres of cultural authority" (DONALD/RATTANSI, 1992, p. 2).

From such a perspective, diversity is always articulated in relation to an apparently stable, homogeneous and largely unexamined "core culture" whose legitimacy is rarely if ever called into question. By contrast, an emphasis on difference rather than diversity leads to a focus on political questions of power and inequality which lead, in turn, to an examination of social relations and material practices rather than vaguely defined notions of identity and experience. Above all, it forces us to examine what "diversity in the city" is being articulated in relation to —destabilising and unsettling the very notion of unitary national cultures and focusing instead on their contested and permeable boundaries. For, as Akhil GUPTA and James FERGUSON (1992) have argued, social and cultural processes now regularly exceed the boundaries of individual nation-states. Our attention as social scientists therefore needs to focus on understanding these increasingly trans-national geographies.

Transnational commodity cultures

Approaching transnationality through the lens of commodity culture involves accepting Appadurai's invitation to trace the "social life of things" as their meanings are inscribed in their forms, uses and trajectories. It is by tracing the social geographies of "things-in-motion", according to Appadurai, that we can best illuminate their human and social context (1986, p. 5). Such an emphasis on transnational commodity cultures helps call into question the very idea of a definitive centre of cultural reference and authority: an unexamined "Britishness", for example, against which everything else is defined as an ethnically-marked "minority" culture.

Appadurai himself offers a striking counterpoint to all of the recent work on "globalisation", with its depressing emphasis on the inevitability of cultural homogenisation. Appadurai's focus on transnational connections leads to a worldview that is much more de-centred. He argues, for example, that: "The United States is no longer the puppeteer of a world system of images but is only one node of a complex transnational construction of imaginary landscapes" (1996, p. 31), or that:

> World systems, regarded especially from the cultural point of view, now emerge as much from Bombay, Tokyo, Rio de Janeiro and Hong Kong as they do from Los Angeles, New York, London and Paris (Appadurai/Breckenridge 1988, p. 2).

An emphasis on transnationality shifts the focus from untenable assumptions about unitary national cultures to an inquisitiveness about the multiple ways in which social differences are articulated across all sorts of boundaries (of class, race, gender, region etc.) —but always articulated through relations of differential power.

To pursue these arguments, let us now turn to some specific examples concerning the transnational geographies of British-Asian culinary culture. As *The Guardian* newspaper asked its readers: "What does this dish say about Britain?" (25 August 1998) —the dish in question being an "Indian" curry. The "politics of curry" to which that article refers have become highly charged as curry is now popularly represented as Britain's "national" dish, replacing previous favourites such as fish and chips, or (less surprisingly perhaps in the context of the recent BSE crisis) roast beef and Yorkshire pudding. A later article in the same newspaper asked rhetorically "What is Britain's great contribution to world cuisine?" (4 November 1999), the answer, again, being curry. And yet the geography of this simple dish is anything but simple. According to most authorities, the word "curry" comes from a Tamil word, "kari", which was adopted by the British in India as a generalised signifier for a range of local masalas —the commodity form embodying complex histories and geographies of imperialism (cf. NARAYAN, 1995). Curry became an increasingly popular dish in Britain following large-scale immigration from the Indian sub-continent in the 1960s, though the classic "Indian" restaurant was in many cases, actually run by Bangladeshis. Subsequent elaborations have seen the humble curry reinvented as a *tandoori* and then as a *balti*, with successive variations appearing on supermarket shelves as well as in restaurants under increasingly exotic names (many of which would not be recognised in India). This is no simple story of a cultural import being stripped of its authenticity through subsequent cultural appropriations (COOK/CRANG, 1996). It goes to the very heart of what constitutes the nation and de-stabilises the very meaning of Britishness.

These complex transnationalities can be further illustrated by a firm like Patak's who might conventionally be represented as a simple immigrant entrepreneurial success story. The firm is transnational in the simple biographical sense, having been established by husband and wife team Kirit and Meena Pathak, following their migration to Britain from Kenya in 1956. From modest beginnings, selling sweets, savoury snacks and spices from a shop on Drummond Street in London, the Pathaks are now one of the richest Asian families in Britain. The firm registered pre-tax profits of £5.5m in 1999, exporting to 44 countries worldwide and supplying a substantial proportion of Britain's "Indian" restaurant trade. According to Kirit Pathak, the transnational biographies of his family are inexorably tied up with the process of product development:

> Although we have highly mechanised production lines, I still regard my tongue, nose and eyes as my real work tools... My wife Meena is responsible for creating the majority of recipes in our product range. Once she has perfected a recipe at home, it's brought into the Product Development kitchen at the factory and completely dissected and then rebuilt.

Their current advertising campaign stresses culinary authenticity, guaranteed by the product's close association with the Pathaks themselves, under the slogan: "Share Patak's passion for India".

By contrast, a rival company like Sharwood's has evolved through very different transnational geographies, though the product is remarkably similar. Founded in the City of London in 1889 by James Allen Sharwood as an importer of curry powders, pickles and chutneys from Bombay and Madras, Sharwood's has found it difficult to shake off its associations with the British Raj. The company was acquired by Rank Hovis McDougall in 1963 and now sells a range of products from China and South-East Asia as well as India. Like Patak's, their current advertising campaign stresses their "passion" for what they produce, but without the same appeals to culinary authenticity. According to a senior brand manager at Sharwood's, this apparent drawback has been turned to advantage as consumers are reassured that the product won't be too exotic, "too ethnic if you like" (personal interview conducted by Philip Crang as part of the current research).

Compared to the richness of these transnational geographies, the literature on culinary culture has tended to get bogged down in an unhelpful opposition between those who deplore the economic exploitation that tends to accompany all such forms of cultural appropriation and those who celebrate the culinary diversity that it apparently represents. The two perspectives are neatly summarised in the following quotations:

> The world on a plate. From Afghani ashak to Zimbabwean zaza, London offers an unrivalled selection of foreign flavours and cuisines. Give your tongue a holiday and treat yourself to the very best meals in the world —all without setting foot outside our fair capital city (Time Out, 16 August 1995, quoted in Cook/Crang, 1996, p. 131).

The celebratory tone of this quotation from a London listings magazine contrasts markedly with the withering tone of this extract from the African American cultural critic, bell hooks: "Within commodity culture, ethnicity becomes spice, seasoning that can liven up the dull dish that is mainstream white culture" (hooks, 1992, p. 21).

The remainder of this chapter aims to go beyond these rather starkly polarised positions and to shift the empirical emphasis from food to fashion. Based on three specific examples, the argument is designed to illustrate the *multiple connections and circuits* that characterise contemporary British-Asian transnationalism. Each example demonstrates different kinds of transnationality: some involving British-Asian entrepreneurs (like Kirit Pathak in the previous example); others with no such direct connections in terms of personal biography. In some cases the transnational connections are established in terms of the sourcing of materials or craft skills like sewing, dyeing and embroidery. In other cases, the transnationality of the product exists in more symbolic terms, through cultural references or imaginary geographies that appeal to consumers' culturally-embedded ideas about the meaning of the Orient, India or the East.

The case studies

The first case study is the young designer Liaqat Al-Rasul, a fashion graduate from the University of Derby whose degree show was sponsored by the British designer Joe Heywood Casey and who recently won a commission from the London department store Liberty's. Liaqat was born in Britain, of Pakistani heritage. He grew up in Wales where his father ran a retail clothing business. Liaqat's own interest in fashion stems from his family background. He describes accompanying his father on buying trips and developing a critical eye for the quality of the workmanship. Once at Derby Liaqat chose to go to the sub-continent to do his industrial placement, but he specifically rejected Pakistan, as having "too many relatives to visit", in favour of a placement at NIFT, the prestigious art college in Delhi.

Liaqat's designs reflect the influence of top Indian designer Ritu Kumar who is widely recognised as a key figure in the revival of the Indian handicraft tradition and the emergence of "Asian chic" (Indian designer fashion drawing on indigenous embroideries and block printing). Liaqat's work uses Indian fabrics and ideas but put together in different ways. For example, one of his outfits is made of recycled fabrics —duvet materials, and packaging cloths which carry the name and address of the delivery site written in Hindi. The stitching on the fabric is traditional Bengali embroidery, a functional running stitch used to recycle old fabrics but used here as a form of decoration. Liaqat talks about his clothes as a critical engagement with multiculturalism: through sewing together many different culturally inflected pieces (paisley print, printed packaging material, traditional Bengali embroidery) or by putting different fabrics alongside each other, he produces an impact which involves a "jarring" or mixing up, reflecting his own understanding of the meaning of "multiculturalism". At the same time Liaqat wants to tell the story of each of these cultural elements. He rejects the "cut and mix" approach of many Western designers to "ethnic" products which dislocates them from any sense of their specific origins.

Liaqat has established a workshop in Delhi (through a contact made via email) and employs local tailors to make up his collection for Liberty's. In interview, Liaqat explained that his identity as British-Pakistani is something he works through in his designs via a discourse of multiculturalism. It is also particularly interesting that he chooses to explore his transnational identity through India —not Pakistan— which brings him, through Ritu Kumar, to an appreciation of "traditional" Indian handicrafts, although he chooses to incorporate these traditions in very different ways from her in his own designs. Liaqat's collection is not aimed at Asian consumers in Britain but at a broader —and more affluent— customer base. His adoption by Liberty also seems significant in relation to the company's transnational history as an emporium of "exotic" fabrics from the East as well as its strong connections with the Arts and Crafts movement. (In an interesting twist to this story, Liaqat has recently started to work with Anokhi, a company whose very different transnational geographies we describe below.)

Our second case study is of a more "traditional" British-Asian firm, Sequinze —the designer off-shoot of Banwait Brothers, a wholesale and retail firm that has sold "Asian" fabric on Southall Broadway in west London for many years. Banwait Bros. was established as a fabric wholesale business in 1967 by three brothers who immigrated to London from India. The business expanded to include three shops in Southall and two in Birmingham before two of the brothers emigrated to Canada in the 1980s where they opened businesses in Vancouver and Toronto. The London part of the business is now run by the remaining brother and his wife plus their two sons and daughter-in-law. Banwait Bros. sell both ready-made clothes and fabrics. While fabrics were originally sourced from India and India remains an important market for particular kinds of fabrics —including specially commissioned hand-embroidered organza— China, Korea and Japan are now important markets for fabrics like chiffons and silks. Their transnational geographies are therefore already quite complex in both biographical and material terms.

Although Banwait's have sold ready-made clothes since the mid-1980s the expansion of their designer wear ranges has been spearheaded by Jasleen, who came to London from India on her marriage to Raj, one of the Banwait brothers, six years ago. The clothes are sold under the Sequinze name, which was chosen to sound "modern" and not traditionally "Asian".

The collection is sold within a separate upstairs gallery at Banwait Bros., styled through references to an Indian heritage with carved wooden chests, chairs and vases. This upper gallery is intended to entice a particular kind of customer - younger Asian women seeking ready-made designer clothes. In January 2000 Jasleen launched her own designer collection, inspired by new fabrics which were imported from China, incorporating traditional dragon and willow pattern designs. Even her *shalwar kameez* (trouser suits) incorporated Chinese-style collars and fastenings. According to their publicity material, Jasleen's designs aim "to combine traditional and modern influences, using embroidery styles that are hundreds of years old to create outfits that have a contemporary cut and design". The range was made up in London rather than in India and promoted through a fashion show at the Cafe de Paris and through an style insert in the style section of the "Asian" newspaper *Eastern Eye*.

Sequinze therefore embodies various kinds of transnationality. While the biographies of those who own the business are transnational, Banwait Brothers reject the discourse of a traditional "family business" with its narrow connotations of ethnic enterprise. Being in the centre of Southall enables Sequinze to cater for a range of different markets beyond the local "Asian" population including those visiting family and friends in Britain or India who shop in Southall while en route to Heathrow airport. Their Indian counterparts have used Southall as a source of imported fabrics from China or Japan which, until recently, were not available in India because of trade restrictions.

The final example concerns the complex history of Anokhi, a company which was originally established as a wholesale operation in the late 1980s to market hand-printed traditional wooden-block designs. The company was set up in India by a British-Indian couple, John and Faith Singh. Faith Singh was the daughter of the Anglican bishop of Nagpur who lived in India until Independence and then returned in the 1960s to explore the commercial potential of Rajasthani textiles. John Singh was a member of the Indian elite, educated at Oxford, who returned to Jaipur to run an experimental farm. Anokhi products were originally sold at Liberty's in London and then became a Monsoon brand in the 1970s. When Monsoon dropped the Anokhi brand in an acrimonious split, three former Monsoon directors set up a new company, called East, in the mid 1990s, capitalising on their knowledge of the Anokhi brand and aiming to broaden Anokhi's British market base. East have now developed into a well-known women's wear chain, with 23 stores across the UK including their flag-ship store in Covent Garden. East's press release explains the "ethnic roots" behind the brand. The clothes are "designed to be individual", for women who want "something a little exotic but also wearable".

In this case, then, East has little biographical connection to India, except via John Singh who is a company director. Their clothes are designed in the UK (except for the Anokhi brand of clothing and furnishings which are imported from Delhi). Their clothes are made up in Indian factories, using local agents (especially "Westernised" Indian women who are valued for their appreciation of the British market). While some of East's clothes have clear Indian influences, others use fabrics and designs from China and Hong Kong. Stylistically, their clothes exhibit varying degrees of dislocation. While the Anokhi brand has clear "Indian" origins, other designs make only generalised references to "the East", as illustrated in their recent publicity brochure which was shot on location in Tunisia. Their clothes have been featured in the "mainstream" British press (the *Daily Telegraph, Good Housekeeping*) and their typical customers are described as "life managers" and "older explorers", with little or no connection to the British-Asian community. Like the previous examples, East demonstrates the complexity of transnational commodity culture, from the sourcing of materials, through design and production, to marketing and final consumption, where different firms may emphasise quite different dimensions of transnationality and occupy different places within British-Asian transnational space.

Conclusion

This chapter has approached the question of "diversity in the city" through the specific lens of (British-Asian) transnational commodity culture. The language of "diversity" has been eschewed in preference for an emphasis on the articulation of difference through specific social relations of power. In the examples discussed, whether in the food or fashion sectors, difference can be seen to emerge not as an inherent property of particular goods or through their direct association with particular migrant communities. Rather, the evidence would suggest, difference emerges as a relational term, through various forms of transnational connection, involving a variety of "players" who may or may not themselves be closely connected to specific transnational communities. The transnational field or social space within which these material practices and relations take shape are, however, always characterised by an uneven distribution of power.

An exploration of the transnational geographies associated with the British-Asian food and fashion sectors helps move the analysis of "diversity in the city" beyond an implicit assumption of unitary national cultures. The case studies have been used to demonstrate the multiple dimensions of these transnational geographies —including the personal and biographical, the sourcing and supply of raw materials, manufacturing and marketing processes, and the symbolic geographies that are drawn out of transnational commodities in specific modes of consumption. It has been argued that looking at transnationalism through the lens of contemporary commodity culture offers new insights into the challenge of living with difference, unsettling the boundaries of "Britishness" and helping to articulate new ways of imagining our cultural and political identities.

Acknowledgements

The research on which this chapter is based was funded by the (UK) Economic and Social Research Council's *Transnational Communities* programme (award no. L214252031) and undertaken in collaboration with Philip Crang and Claire Dwyer, with research assistance from Suman Prinjha. Thanks also to the organisers of the conference at which an earlier version of this paper was delivered and particularly to Eric Florence for his thoughtful and penetrating remarks as discussant.

References

APPADURAI, A. (ed.) (1986): *The social life of things*. University of Cambridge Press, Cambridge.
APPADURAI, A. (1998): *Modernity at large: cultural dimensions of globalization*. University of Minnesota Press, Minneapolis.
APPADURAI, A.; BRECKENRIDGE, C.A. (1988): "Why public culture?" *Public Culture* 1, pp. 5-9.
BASCH, L.; GLICK SCHILLER, N.; SZANTON-BLANC, C. (1994): *Nations unbound: transnational projects, postcolonial predicaments and deterritorialized nation-states*. Gordon & Breach, Langhorne, PA.
BRAH, A. (1992): "Difference, diversity and differentiation". In: *"Race", culture and difference*, ed. J. Donald and A. Rattansi. Sage, London, pp. 126-45.

BRAH, A. (1996): *Cartographies of diaspora.* Routledge. London.
COOK, I.; CRANG, P. (1996): "The world on a plate: culinary culture, displacement and geographical knowledges". In: *Journal of Material Culture* 1, pp. 131-53.
DONALD, J.; RATTANSI, A. (eds.) (1992): *"Race", culture and difference.* Sage, London.
GLICK-SCHILLER, N.; BASCH, L.; BLANC-SZANTON, C. (1994): "Transnationalism: a new analytical framework for understanding migration". In: *Towards a transnational perspective on migration,* ed. N. Glick-Schiller, L. Basch and C. Blanc-Szanton. New York Academy of Sciences, New York: pp. 201-16.
GUPTA, A.; FERGUSON, J. (1992): "Beyond 'culture': space, identity, and the politics of difference". In: *Cultural Anthropology* 7, pp. 6-23.
JACKSON, P. 1999. "Commodity cultures: the traffic in things". In: *Transactions of the Institute of British Geographers* 24, pp. 95-108.
JACKSON, P.; TAYLOR, J. (1996): "Geography and the cultural politics of advertising". In: *Progress in Human Geography* 20, pp. 356-71.
MARX, K. (1867; republished 1977): *Capital, Volume 1.* Vintage Books, New York.
MITCHELL, K. (1997): "Different diasporas and the hype of hybridity". In: *Environment and Planning D: Society and Space* 15, pp. 533-53.
NARAYAN, U. (1995): "Eating cultures: incorporation, identity and Indian food". In: *Social Identities* 1, pp. 63-86.
ONG, A.; NONINI, D. (eds.) (1997): *Ungrounded empires: the cultural politics of modern Chinese transnationalism.* Routledge, New York.
PORTES, L.; GUARNIZO, L.E.; LANDOLT, P. (1999): "Introduction: pitfalls and promise of an emergent research field". In: *Ethnic and Racial Studies* 22, pp. 217-37.
ROUSE, R. (1991): "Mexican migration and the social space of postmodernism". In: *Diaspora: a journal of transnational studies* 1, pp. 8-23.
SLATER, D. (1997): *Consumer culture and modernity.* Polity Press, Cambridge.
SMITH, M.P.; GUARNIZO, L.F. (eds.) (1998): *Transnationalism from below.* Transaction Publishers, New Brunswick, NJ.
VERTOVEC, S. (1999): "Conceiving and researching transnationalism". In: *Ethnic and Racial Studies* 22, pp. 447-62.